To Lois

Best wishes from —

Patricia Prattis Jennings

IN ONE ERA

AND

OUT THE OTHER

ESSAYS ON CONTEMPORARY LIFE

Pat Jennings

11/13

ISBN: 0615849903
ISBN-13: 9780615849904
Library of Congress Control Number: 2013948202
Harbinger Publishing

Author's Note

In One Era and Out the Other is a compilation of writings from 1996 through mid 2013, arranged in chronological order. Except for "Hold Your Fire!" those in Group 1 were published in the *Pittsburgh Post-Gazette* between 1996 and 2008. The second, much larger group, were written between 2008 and 2013 and published online as *Pat's Ponderings* at SquareSpace.com.

Although the essays were written within the last two decades, there are occasional references to what life was like during the era in which I grew up, when power steering was state-of-the-art in automotive technology, and a woman still needed her husband's signature to get a credit card.

My, how times have changed.

Patricia Prattis Jennings, June 2013

TABLE OF CONTENTS

Foreword

When you grow up subbing in the summertime for vacationing employees at the nationally circulated *Pittsburgh Courier* of which your father is the world-traveled editor, then go on have a career full of firsts during more than forty years as the keyboardist with the Pittsburgh Symphony Orchestra, circumnavigating the globe yourself, what is left to do after retiring? If your name is Patricia Prattis Jennings, you might settle down to analyze the world and offer a unique philosophy of daily life. Has anyone else written about "those gray, drizzly mornings when it would have been easier for O. J. to find the real killer than find a parking space in downtown Pittsburgh"?

Not everyone can distill an amusing tale out of hairdos...food courts...broccoli...introducing your husband to your new computer...SUV's...but everyone can relate.

And just when she has you chuckling, Jennings turns on a dime to offer a pointed reality check on Trent Lott's lavish devotion to Strom Thurmond, which she does with style, carrying the reader along on sheer eloquence that recognizes nothing as "politically correct."

You wouldn't know what her complexion or ethnicity might be until you read the first-hand recollection of a girl who grew up in Pittsburgh on her family's first trip south by rail, where she saw, with her own innocent eyes, the fabled water fountains – one for White and one for Colored – as she and her family made their way to the "Colored" waiting room" of the Birmingham railroad station.

The values that unapologetically infuse this collection are universal – or almost. It's good to know that *someone* in the 21st century finds it unacceptable behavior for a man to take his wife to a sex club and ask her to perform with him in public...even if a certain Republican businessman and would be candidate for the U. S. Senate considers that a good mite more acceptable than adultery.

If Harry Golden, publisher of the *Carolina Israelite*, and author of *Only in America*, had been born a woman in Pittsburgh in 1941, he might have written this mix of memoir, humor, and commentary. Half a century from now, *In One Era and Out the Other* will provide a fascinating insight into the travails of daily life at the turn of the century (this century). But those of us who around now can get an early peek at how we will look to our literate great-grandchildren.

Charles A. Rosenberg, researcher-biographer,
Milwaukee, Wisconsin

PART I
1996-2008

1

A Reader's Dilemma

This was the first of my articles to appear in a Pittsburgh Post-Gazette *feature called* Life Support *whose topics covered a wide range of subjects.*

The hyperventilating you hear in the background might be me, succumbing to one final attack of reader frustration.

How does one squeeze into the day all the things that should be done – exercise, flossing, drinking eight glasses of water, not to mention going to work and fulfilling familial and social obligations – and still have time to deal with the mountain of reading matter that comes sailing across the threshold?

Do you suffer from this malady? Do you have stacks of half-read books beside your bed, piles of "must-read" periodicals cluttering your den or office? Do you have to sprint past bookstores, heart rate elevated, eyes averted? Yours is a classic case of Reader's Dilemma.

There are days when I can't do justice even to the morning *Post-Gazette*. I attack the paper, gobbling headlines, whipping from page to page, trying to absorb the gist of George Will's grumbling or Ellen Goodman's insights, in the vain hope that I'll have the time to go back and read them in their entirety. And then someone airily asks me, "Did you see such-and-such in last Sunday's *New York Times?*" adding, "You *do* get the *Times?*"

I love *The New York Times*, but the last time I was able to read a Sunday edition from beginning to end was when I had gallbladder surgery in 1981.

For thirty years I've subscribed to *New York* magazine (have I ever *not* had to say, "No, *not* the *New Yorker*"?) but recently cancelled the subscription because the contents were evolving in a way I found distasteful. They started printing the F-word. Harrumph. So, with *New York out of the way, and primarily the Post-Gazette, Time,* and *Newsweek* to get through (plus a few monthlies like *Bon Appétit* and *Martha Stewart Living)* I thought, "Maybe I can get some books read." That worked pretty well until a tempting offer arrived from *Food and Wine* (huge savings!), followed by an even more alluring one for *Conde Nast Traveler,* and finally one from *Moneysworth,* which promised to make dealing with everyday finances a breeze and save our household thousands of dollars a year.

These troves of information are now filling up our mailbox, along with *Discover, Symphony, Remedy, Ebony, Pittsburgh, Nutrition Action, Wine Spectator,* and, of course, *Writer's Digest,* a cache of wisdom for people like me who believe one can learn how to write by reading a magazine.

Periodical in hand, I rush to the john, to the doctor's office, to the beauty shop (talk about taking coals to Newcastle), even to the bathtub, trying to reserve the precious few minutes before I drop off to sleep at midnight for whatever book(s) I'm reading.

For me, one of the joys of travel is being able to read uninterrupted (sort of) on planes, trains, and buses. During a recent airport layover, I decided to treat myself to the issue of *Vanity Fair* with Emma Thompson's picture on the cover, and a dishy piece about the Macaulay Culkin clan inside. But there, right next to *Vanity Fair* was a magazine I had never seen before. It seemed so right, so timely, considering this problem with which I've been struggling. The magazine is aptly named – *Going Bonkers!*

Going Bonkers is a useful magazine, certainly, chock-full of advice on how to handle life's little ups and downs, but it didn't mention one thing about curing Reader's Dilemma; it only added to the problem – and I still haven't finished reading about Emma.

Why do I turn reading into such an obligation? It's simple; I don't want to miss anything, and I fantasize that if I read fast enough and long enough, I can read it all. Some people want to have it all; I want to *know* it all.

In truth, reading is one of my greatest pleasures, Reader's Dilemma a malady from which I hope never to recover. How unfortunate are those who cannot, or will not, read. They do not know how impoverished they are.

Now, if you'll excuse me, Martha Stewart and I are off to the tub.

2

Getting My Comeuppance

I did a horrible thing. After waiting several weeks for a thank-you note from a couple who had been guests at our dinner table, I sat down and wrote *them* a thank-you note, telling them how happy we were that they took time from their busy schedules to share an evening with us. I didn't think up that atrocity all by myself. Years before someone had done it to my mother – written to thank her for accepting their hospitality. I remember thinking it was an appalling thing for the offended hostess to do, but also wonderfully wicked.

My jab at our friends' breach of etiquette brought a swift and sure reaction. They called and invited us to dinner at a fancy restaurant. We accepted. Feeling appropriately contrite, and thus one-upped, I ordered flowers delivered to their door the next day.

Because of that painful episode, I am permanently chastened. I will *never* do that again. But I would like to ask you this: Do you believe that simply uttering "Thank you for a lovely evening," as you're walking out your hosts' front door – after they have spent several days planning a menu, shopping, cooking, cleaning house, setting a lovely table and selecting just the right wines – is sufficient? If your answer is "Yes," I hope you might consider rethinking your position.

I'm not talking about an impromptu or couple-of-times-a-week meal at your best friends' or your sister's house. I'm referring to the sit-down gathering, the "perfect little dinner," as Miss Manners puts it, where six or eight people, who don't see each other very often, share the same table. (Parties are a different matter. The larger the crowd, the less necessary the note; the larger the crowd, the less special you are.)

A generation ago, this type of correspondence was called a "bread and butter" note. Call it what you like. According to Miss Manners, "It's *still* necessary, and not just according to finicky old snippets." It's the least you can do when you have been honored with a dinner invitation. You know how hard *you* work to pull off one of those "she seems to do everything with such ease..." dinner gatherings – unless, of course, you'd sooner set your hair on fire than even attempt such a thing.

A thank-you note reinforces the uttered "Thank you" and demonstrates that you thought about the pleasant time you enjoyed for perhaps another day after you turned out of your hosts' driveway. And, Miss Manners suggests that at the very least your thank-you note will give your hosts a lift when their mail comes and they discover it's not all bills and catalogs.

If writing anything other than a grocery list is something you abhor, a thank-you phone call the next day is better than sinking into a black hole, never to be heard from again. Or, on your next trip to the mall, pick up printed notes that say it all for you. Everything from

"Thanks for your gracious hospitality" to "Great group, great grub." All you have to do is sign it.

If your reaction to all of this is "I'm too busy to write notes, " or "I'm just no good at writing notes," or "It's just too much trouble," you might consider that the people who invited you could have been too busy, not good enough at it, or not willing to trouble themselves by inviting you in the first place.

While I'm pontificating about thank-you notes, I'd like to mention a related matter – the hostess gift, a small something you take to the hostess in response to the honor of being invited. It doesn't have to be elaborate. A bottle of wine, a small bouquet, or cocktail napkins will do nicely.

As is true of most of the rules of old-fashioned etiquette, these niceties boil down to one thing: the Golden Rule. Treat other people the way you'd like to be treated yourself, and think about how much you appreciated the last thank-you note – or any other mail that didn't say "Bulk Rate" – the mailman brought you.

3

Lesson Learned

One day last spring, I did something really stupid. It was one of those gray, drizzly mornings when it would have been easier for O. J. to find the real killer than find a parking space in downtown Pittsburgh.

There's a parking lot near my workplace when, even if the "FULL" sign is on, there's space in the driveway for four cars to station themselves until a few customers drive out and the sign changes to "Please take ticket."

I pulled in at the end of the line, hoping my car's rear end wouldn't obstruct pedestrian traffic and trigger a "Move it, lady" from the motorcycle cop across the street. There was a big space between the two cars in front of me, and I wondered how I could induce the closer driver to move forward. I couldn't see anyone in the driver's seat so I tiptoed to the car, peered inside and found the fellow dozing on his lowered seat-back. I decided against tapping on his window – I didn't want to startle him – so I got back in my car and waited a few minutes. Thinking.

I cannot tell you what convinced me my next move would be a better solution. I decided to bump his car with my car. Not a crunch. Just a teeny little…boop.

7

"WHY'D YOU HIT MY CAR??? WHAT'S THE MATTER WITH YOU??? ARE YOU CRAZY???

At that point I should have said, "I'm so sorry," and leaped from my car to help him look for the, uh, damage. But in true '90s style, I matched him jab for jab. I knew there was no damage, but he was determined to examine his bumper, and he threatened to call the police if I didn't back up.

"And just what are you gonna tell them?" I taunted.

"That YOU HIT MY CAR!" he bellowed.

"Why would they believe you?" I countered. "Your car's not damaged!" It went on like that until the "Please take ticket" sign forced a cease-fire.

I realize that what I did could have gotten me into big trouble, either with any weapons he might have been packing, or with my insurance company.

Granted, the guy was rudely awakened from his snooze. But the speed and ferocity of his reaction, even in this Age of Rage, was way out of proportion. We've all bumped or been bumped by other drivers. That's why those things on our cars are called *bumpers*. But too many of us seem primed to pounce on our fellow man, or woman. Ask someone at the movies to stop blabbing, and be happy to escape with your life.

Why have we become so angry? Food additives? Chemicals in our drinking water?

Assuming that my theories are as valid as anyone else's, maybe we're just fed up with our lack of power. We can't change our out-of-control health system. Corporate mega-mergers and layoffs make us feel increasingly impotent. Our children are shooting each other. And school administrators, having lost track of their common sense, dole out ludicrous zero-tolerance punishments to the six-year-old who brings a plastic toy ax to school or hugs his classmate.

Having little recourse, we vent our rage on strangers – who can't fire us and who probably won't shoot us or follow us home and slaughter our families. (*That* we leave to family members and neighbors.) But the problem with rage is that, while we're trying to punish those who offend us, we end up feeling worse, we end up being the bad guy.

Although we can't eliminate frustrating situations from our lives, there is something that can help us deal with our rage. Being enraged is a choice, made in a split second, but a choice nonetheless.

The next time something happens that would ordinarily make you fly off the handle, force yourself to react differently. Face-to-face with a grouch? Disarm him with a cheerful, "Hi!" Behind a slowpoke in the checkout line? Try those deep breathing exercises you've been meaning to add to your health regimen.

Instead of reacting with anger, slam on your emotional brakes and take a deep breath. Inhale. Exhale. Later, when the incident is behind you, you'll be pleased with the manner in which you handled it and remember it with pride instead of renewed rage. You will have experienced the best power of all, power over yourself.

4

If the Shoes Don't Fit

This one sounds like something from the nineteenth century. The earth has done several revolutions since it was written. Some of the shoe brands I mention no longer exist, and the high-heeled, pointy-toed shoes of my youth have come back with higher heels and pointier toes than I might have thought possible. And to compound the insanity, someone decided that holding high heel races for charity would be a good idea. I hope the orthopedic surgeons-in-training are prepared to start raking in the dough.

Luxuriating in the tub, stealing a few minutes for the Sunday paper, I notice in the 'Style" section a feature on the latest shoe styles. At the top of the page there's a sturdy, thick-soled loafer with a pizazzy Dalmatian-spotted vamp. I think, "Wow, the guys are getting racy," and I tease my conservative husband, "Honey, you should get yourself a pair of these." When my gaze shifts to the other photo on the page, I come to a startling realization – these are *women's* shoes!

What in the world is going on in the minds of designers? Why are they foisting upon us these grotesque receptacles passing as shoes? Gargantuan heels, tire-tread soles, gladiator straps, Ben Franklin buckles, zippers and hardware – anything you can think of that's unfeminine – can be found on the new crop of women's footwear.

A few years back, just when I thought I had seen it all, I began to notice females from our local art school lurking about the downtown streets fixed up like characters from the Munsters – black-dyed hair with fuchsia highlights, terrifying eye makeup and, to tie it all together, bubble-toed combat boots. Knowing that men find women in high heels sexy, I wondered what sort of fellow would find this ghoulish look a turn-on and then realized it would be the fellow across the street sporting a Kelly-green Mohawk, dressed in baggy pants with the crotch at knee level. A union made in heaven.

But the shoes I'm seeing in mainstream establishments are supposed to be for normal women – women, I hope, like me. Although some of my smart-alecky friends think I'm related to Imelda Marcos, there really are gaps in my shoe wardrobe. And, always the optimist, I visit a shoe store expecting to find just the style I need – a delicate, strappy sandal to wear with summer frocks, a sleek black sling-back, with a bit of a heel, to go with slacks. But they usually don't have what I'm looking for. Instead, I'm greeted by displays of shoes that only a dominatrix or the mother of the designer could love.

Fashion watchers tell us that the new styles are created with comfort in mind. Maybe so, but most of them look pretty uncomfortable – hot and heavy, like something you'd wear on a moon walk to counteract weightlessness.

For years I've resisted going to the traditional comfort shoe lines – the Selbys and Naturalizers, the Cobbies and even the not-so-dowdy Easy Spirits. When I was young we called them "old lady" shoes. But if this trend continues, I won't have much choice.

In the antediluvian days of my youth, when a dainty foot was the standard, we girls went to painful lengths to make our feet look small – though not to the extreme of binding them like our Chinese sisters of yore. We squeezed our toes into needle-nosed pumps with four-inch stiletto heels so sharp they punched holes in our mothers' linoleum kitchen floors. Anything wider than a triple-A or an ultra-chic quad betrayed one's peasant roots.

Those Barbie Doll pumps were usually uncomfortable and often inflicted noticeable pain on the wearer. Many times mine ended up being carried rather than worn. But, discomfort notwithstanding, those shoes were feminine – if one could manage to walk in them without hobbling or grimacing.

Having watched the tide of fashion turn, years after year, with numbing predictability, I realize that these experiments in differentness are meant for the young, for those who haven't lived through it all several times before. How many skirt lengths can there be? How many heel heights, widths and shapes? While I ponder those questions, I'll have to make do with just being a spectator at this late-century fashion spectacle.

For years I had forgotten there was such a person as the neighborhood shoemaker, thinking he had disappeared along with the bouffant hairdo. But lately, he and I have rediscovered each other as I leave in his care shoes that would have been considered a lost cause until recently. I used to wear shoes until the heels wore down nearly to the quick, and then pitch them into the Goodwill bag. Now, I find myself recycling the hopeless cases, praying they'll hold together a few months longer while I wait for femininity, and sanity, to return to the shoe business.

Until then, I'm keeping the Goodwill bag handy for raiding, reinforcing my ties to the village cobbler, and using the money I save to buy some shares of Selby stock.

5

The Hair's the Thing

On Inauguration Day, the *Washington Post's* Sally Quinn, veteran of many years of Washington blowouts, suggested in an NPR interview that it didn't much matter what you were wearing to one of the many balls, because these shindigs are so crowded that no one would even see you from the neck down. "The only thing that really matters, that might be seen," she said, "is your hair."

There it is. Sad to say, it's true that whether you're at an inaugural ball or your high school reunion, what counts most is not what designer fashions might adorn your form or your feet, or even what magic has been worked on your eyes and complexion by Shiseido or Lancôme. If your hair is, as we said in high school, "in a trick," you might as well forget it. You won't look good and you certainly won't feel good.

A couple of months ago I spent $162 getting my hair done. If I had been miraculously transformed, à la Oprah and her resident stylemeister Andre Walker, I would have considered it money well spent. Had I been greeted by the cashier at the salon, my husband, or anyone with, "Your hair looks fabulous," I'd have felt some justification for my budgetary recklessness. But I thought my hair looked rather pathetic.

First of all, there wasn't much of it left. While I was engrossed in a weekly newsmagazine, most of my hair had quietly hit the floor. Secondly, little pieces of what remained began to stick out in odd places, some of which appeared even before my head and my pillow had mixed it up during the night.

Is there something about my hair that makes finding a great hairdo like the search for the Philosopher's Stone? Off and on, over, say, five years, I noticed several women whose hair always looked magnificent. And darned if it didn't turn out that they were all using the same stylist. My hope was restored. Had I found my man? I could hardly wait until business hours to make an appointment with this wizard.

Well, when I went to see him, he must have given his magical powers the day off, because he sent me away with a wispy "do" that didn't even hold up against the breeze between my driveway and my house. And by evening, my hair was so droopy you'd think I had spent the day over a steam table. In his mailbox a few days later he found my photo with a note: "This is how I looked the evening you did my hair."

But this *artiste* and others of his ilk are unrepentant, impervious to our dissatisfaction, and react as if we are simply not hip enough to know what looks good. They flatter us into submission, talking us into costly procedures we don't know we need until we were seated at their stations.

This fellow cajoled me into having my hair colored. "It'll get rid of the gray," he counseled. I had so little gray hair, no one had ever even noticed it, and it didn't

15

bother me at all. But, as if in a trance, I took the bait and let him do the color. He neglected to mention that the color job would be an additional $50 – FIFTY DOLLARS! – for a bit of brown goop, some of which went onto my hair, but most of which went down the drain.

So let's see: $49 for the cut, $50 for the color, $10 for a conditioner, and $30 for the wash and style. Worth every penny you say? Hah! If you could have seen me, you'd have thought I'd really had one put over on me. And to add to the injury, the salon, in a fancy downtown hotel, doesn't validate parking. So, along with another $8.25 for parking and a $15 tip, I was out $162.25. My husband and I could have spent a night at the hotel with breakfast thrown in for less than that.

A woman's hair is the key to her good looks, and many a bargain-conscious female who will pore over her Sunday paper cutting out coupons for 25 cents off a box of Rice-A-Roni will part with extraordinary amounts of hard-earned cash to pay for a hairdo. And, despite years of disappointments, we never lose our optimism. Our next hairdo – or hair stylist – will be the one who reveals the ravishing creature underneath all of those bad hair days.

As our mothers told us, our hair is our crowning glory and, whether we're walking around in Aerosoles or Manolo Blahniks, Gap or Gucci, we know that "the hair's the thing." And we have to keep in mind that that elusive "to die for" hairstyle, when found, might be the

only part of us that anyone will see at the next inaugural
ball.

6

A Matter of Taste

Picking my way through the crowded food court of a downtown shopping center, I noticed a young male office type seated in front of a Styrofoam container of Chinese food. He hadn't begun to eat; he was carefully extracting the broccoli from his moo goo gai pan or whatever it was and placing it in the lid of the container. Not for a minute did I think he was saving the best for last. Like George Bush the Elder, this guy hates broccoli.

Does anyone know for sure why some people hate broccoli so intensely? Body chemistry? Allergy? Were the broccoli haters forced to eat it as children? Maybe their mothers insisted that they become members of the Clean Plate Club, denying them permission to leave the table until every bit of the green mush set before them was consumed. And how often were they admonished, "Eat it! Children are starving in Europe"?

Like spinach, which has attained a status and popularity that would have been unimaginable in my youth, broccoli has made a breathtaking leap from steam table goop to main ingredient in sizzling stir-fries, velvety soups, and the crudité tray of the calorie- and cholesterol-conscious.

18

Nevertheless, there are people who still won't eat broccoli; in fact, they won't eat *any* vegetable. They'll eat a slab of grilled cow meat or charred pig flesh – creates a different image when put that way, eh? – and a heap of greasy fries, but wouldn't touch a crispy salad or a wicked platter of deep-fried zucchini even if threatened with execution. I have to wonder about the state of their insides. A healthy body needs vegetables.

Close behind the broccoli haters are the seafood-phobic. Some of them won't even eat the most heavenly of the *fruits de mer*, shrimp and lobster. Good. That leaves more for me.

At the top of their list of nasties is the dreaded anchovy. If you are anchovy-averse, this will give you the willies: Many a master chef uses anchovies to flavor some of your favorite dishes. You wouldn't suspect it, and he isn't going to tell you. But that fascinating bit of trivia was divulged in the pages of *Bon Appétit*. I saw it with my own eyes and had to chuckle.

Then there are those whose minds are closed – they've never tasted it, whatever it happens to be, and they never will. Whether it's Chinese food, Mexican food, or any other generally popular cuisine, if it wasn't served to them at home in the '50s and '60s, when the most exciting items on their dinner tables were meat loaf and mashed potatoes, they're not about to begin experimenting now.

My husband is a dream to cook for. No wife could have a more appreciative spouse. He routinely says, "That was very good, dear" even if I've served him something a tad peculiar when a recipe didn't turn out as expected. But even he draws the line at two things: organ meats – no liver or sweetbreads, none of my giblet gravy on Thanksgiving – and no bivalve mollusks – oysters, clams, or mussels, fried, steamed or ("You'd have to kill me first!") raw. Anchovies? Forget it.

When we have company for dinner it's always interesting to see what goes back to the kitchen uneaten. One expects finicky behavior from little kids, who spend most of mealtime saying, "Eeeeew!" and picking out all the yucky things like red cabbage and radicchio. They eschew anything that isn't a grilled cheese sandwich or pizza. But, in thirty-odd years of feeding adults, I have been surprised at the mountains of mushrooms, piles of peppers, and buckets of broccoli I've scraped down the black hole in my kitchen sink.

Truly, there is no accounting for taste. On our recent visit to Argentina, we were made aware of a tea-like drink called maté, which is hugely popular. You see people young and old wandering around the shopping malls sipping maté from a special gourd-like cup held in one hand with a thermos stashed under their other arm to refill their cups. I tasted the stuff. It's TERRIBLE! Tastes like liquid pipe tobacco. Might even be worse than broccoli.

Unfortunately for my figure, there's not much you could put in front of me to eat or drink that I wouldn't consume, or at least sample. I figure that if millions of people around the world are scarfing down sushi and calamari and moussaka, considering that my hips seem determined to expand anyway, why shouldn't I avail myself of every opportunity for corresponding gastronomic growth?

I ask that while realizing that even I have to draw a line somewhere. I prefer that you not serve me head-cheese or haggis, blood sausage, squid ink, or pigs' ears. And please don't whip me up any coffee-avocado milk-shakes – even if you did get the recipe from the latest issue of *Gourmet* magazine. I'll take vanilla.

7

Am I Being Replaced?

I wrote this in my husband's voice as I imagined his reaction to my relationship with my new PC.

Her new computer arrived today. She's been threatening for months to replace her old machine.

But she's put it off, partly because of the expense, but also because she doesn't look forward to the agony of installing and learning a new system.

She's not the only one dreading the agony. I live with her and this contraption. I don't use it, nor do I ever intend to. I've gotten along fine all these years using snail-mail and the encyclopedia. Why should I subject myself to this new assortment of aggravations? A few interesting things come out of her office, but mostly what comes out, especially when she's trying to connect with a human at Technical Support, is a gnashing of teeth and volleys of unprintable language.

I sometimes wonder: If she had to choose between me and the computer, which of us would get to stay? Her computer is her closest associate. She bounces out of bed in the morning and makes a beeline for her office. Bleary-eyed at midnight, she has to finish just one more e-mail, and when she blows through the door in the dead of winter, she rushes into her office, coattails flying.

Living with an e-mailer is like having the mailman deliver a dozen letters a day that have to be answered IMMEDIATELY because the sender is poised at the other end of a cyber-tunnel, ready to snatch the reply as it zooms out of the chute.

She doesn't talk much on the phone anymore – says it's intrusive. After all, how can you talk on the phone when you spend all your spare time writing e-mail? Vacations are planned via e-mail. Shopping is done via e-mail. It wouldn't surprise me if entire governments were organized via e-mail. She could be elected president of a small country without telling me. I'd hear it on the six o'clock news.

When she's cooking, she rushes into her office every few minutes to poke a few keys on the computer. I've offered to put a hot plate in there to save her some steps, but she claims that the running back and forth burns calories.

Every so often, when her conscience is bothering her, she goes to her piano. She has actually practiced for as long as three-and-a-half minutes before thinking of something she MUST do at the computer. I hear a few scales, a few seconds of silence, and then, here she comes, tearing around the corner and through the kitchen like the Road Runner.

There are some things she will interrupt her e-mailing to do: Bathe, sleep, and eat, although I've seen her eat while e-mailing. She hasn't yet figured out how to rig up the computer near the bathtub. There, she settles for simply reading e-mail, the epic printouts of minutiae churned out by her girlfriends. That done, she frantically scans the morning paper. And within minutes she's back at the machine, still toweling herself dry, e-mailing articles all over the place.

I've managed to carve out a solitary little life for myself that doesn't require her participation. I organize my CDs and clip articles from back issues of *Discover* magazine. I immerse myself in video courses on Greek history and spend time in the yard looking at the birds and wondering why everyone else's grass looks better than mine. She's hardly aware that we have a yard. I rake, mow, and take out my frustrations by hurling brooms at the squirrels that steal food from the bird feeder. She came out one day long enough to say, "Gee, we have a whole new crop of brooms!"

There are ways I could get her attention. I could yell "Fire!" except that I'm no good at yelling. I could try falling down the steps carrying the recycling bin. That's guaranteed to make her look up from her keyboard. I can take her out to dinner – alone. Can't involve too many other people or I risk being submerged in a sea of computer gab and feeling as out of it as a ballerina at a truck pull.

But I shouldn't complain. She's having fun, and it amuses me to watch her engaged in this love affair with the new technology while I, the Luddite, am content to court the muses of ancient history.

If something good is coming out of this it's that often, when she does emerge from behind her computer screen, she's waving pages of recipes. That means she might cook something for dinner that doesn't read, "Heat five minutes. Stir. Heat five more minutes." Within seconds she has downloaded six marinades for flank steak and five variations on raspberry vinaigrette. She'll never have to buy another cookbook.

On the Britcom *As Time Goes By*, about a couple who are reunited after thirty-eight years of living other lives, Lionel becomes peeved with Jean's preoccupation with her new computer. Noticing him reading a section of the paper he usually ignores, she asks him, "What are you reading?" "The lonely hearts column," he answers. "I figure you're going to marry that thing eventually, and I'm going to need some companionship."

I don't expect to be looking for a new wife any time soon. This one, with all her peculiarities, is too full of surprises for me to consider trading her in. And besides, she occasionally gets money for the product of her mechanical monster – and takes *me* out to dinner.

8

Piling On

In a recent commentary on a Pittsburgh radio station, the station CEO treated us to his opinion regarding Trent Lott's ill-considered remarks about Strom Thurmond at the superannuated geezer's 100th birthday celebration.

Unhappy about the explosive reaction to Lott's adulation of Thurmond, general manager Robert W. Dickey patronizingly advised the "agitated civil rights folks" to "live and let live" and "get over the mean-spirited piling on."

I don't think he realized that his last admonition could be taken in two ways. In case he's reading this, I'd like to share with him a few examples of a kind of "mean-spirited piling on" by which my family and I and millions of others were affected by dyed-in-the-wool segregationists like Trent Lott's idol Strom Thurmond.

When I was growing up in Pittsburgh, every African-American out-of-towner who came to visit my father on business had to stay in my parents' home because "colored people" weren't welcome in downtown hotels.

When my family visited Tuskegee Institute in Alabama in the '50s, my father chose to pay for a private drawing room on the train rather than expose his wife

26

and young daughter – me – to the insult of the Jim Crow cars relegated to "colored people." When we arrived at the train station in Birmingham, I saw, with my own innocent eyes, the fabled water fountains – one for White and one for Colored – near the "Colored" waiting room.

In the '30s, when my mother worked downtown for the Pennsylvania Department of Public Assistance, she could not try on a garment in any department store near her place of employment. And when her white co-workers went off to lunch at some of the nicer downtown restaurants, she could not go with them, because blacks weren't permitted. In most movie theaters, my mother and her kind were limited to the last row of the balcony, reserved for "Colored."

We had to live with these indignities or risk nasty scenes, even arrest. But the radio commentator might have preferred it if, all along, the pesky civil rights activists who struggled to open public accommodations had adopted his suggested philosophy of "live and let live."

His editorial went on to describe Strom Thurmond as "one of the nation's most influential public servants, a kingmaker who influenced the history of the political South." Thank God he didn't influence it any more than he did. We've endured just about as much of his kind of influence, of his kind of "piling on" as we care to.

During the '50s, when I was in grade school, too many educated blacks had to settle for jobs as sleeping car porters or elevator operators. The rest had to settle for jobs as janitors, and maids and perform other kinds of menial work. There were no black teachers in the public schools, no salespeople or cashiers in even the lowliest establishments that served white people, no policemen, except in black neighborhoods, no firemen.

The majority of black city employees were garbage men, because no one else was desperate enough to be recruited to dump, on even the hottest summer day, barrels of stinking household refuse into burlap tarpaulins to be hauled to waiting trucks.

I wonder how the commentator would feel if everything in American society had been arranged to remind him that he is considered inferior, lower than an animal. (And if that sounds like exaggeration, think of how many dogs and horses were kissed in the movies over the years by white women, who, if they had instead been required to kiss a Negro, such scandalous behavior would have caused a revolution across this land, especially in the South.)

During World War II, my late father, P. L. Prattis, was one of the primary architects of the *Pittsburgh Courier's* "Double V" campaign, which sought to gain equal treatment – victory – at home and in the military for black soldiers who, although required to fight and die for their country, could not expect to be treated as equal citizens when they came back home.

They couldn't live where they wanted to live, they couldn't work where they wanted to work, and many other givens of American life, which we now take for granted, were denied them. If Strom Thurmond had

had his way, and certainly if he had become president, that sorry situation might never have changed.

I'm sure the commentator realizes that if Strom Thurmond had had his way, I would certainly never have become a member of the Pittsburgh Symphony Orchestra nor would I have been accepted at Carnegie Tech (Carnegie Mellon University).

And to this day, although I have traveled the world, garnered ovations in distant lands and been presented with honors undreamed of in my youth, why is it that when I go into a supermarket in certain neighborhoods I still get the feeling that people are looking at me wondering, "What is she doing in *here*?"

But according to the editorial, I and my kind become "unduly agitated" when a stinging reminder of former outrages crashes into our consciousness. We are "piling on." We should "live and let live."

Declarations like this prove, more than anything, that some white people are obtuse when evaluating matters of race. Why else would so many of them be insisting that "Trent Lott misspoke," and that he is not a white supremacist. If he isn't a white supremacist, I'd like to know what the heck he is.

9

Whither the SUV?

I wrote this shortly after buying my first SUV, a Hyundai Santa Fe, when the SUV was still on the ascent and the subject of much controversy.

I find it interesting that while half of my fellow citizens are sputtering and fuming about SUVs, the other half are buying them up at a staggering rate. And manufacturers you might think wouldn't be caught uttering the words SUV have thrown their hats into the ring. A Porsche SUV? Look under "Cayenne."

If SUVs are such a blight on society, how do you account for the furious activity in the SUV market?

Let me first say that I drive an SUV – of moderate price and size. I don't need a stepladder to get into it. Until now, I had thought that the most repugnant thing about me was my snoring, from which my husband has had to escape periodically, in the middle of the night, pillow in hand. But I have learned that I belong to that most vile category of human, those who drive SUVs.

Unlike ethnic and religious groups that are protected by the strictures of political correctness, it's still OK to target fat people, people who smoke, and the newest menace to society – the SUV driver.

There are two factors that purportedly tick people off about SUVs. One is that they use an unfair share of our precious fuel. But the way Americans squander natural resources, more per capita than any other place on Earth, it seems a little disingenuous of the self-appointed guardians of the pump, like the "What would Jesus drive?" busybodies, to pick only on the drivers of SUVs.

The other is the dreaded "rollover." I don't doubt that SUVs have rolled over, but bad things can happen on the road in any vehicle driven poorly or when your number is up.

I suspect that the SUV war is not really about safety or economy. It's a political battle, another way for the haves and have-nots to have at each other. To the SUV-averse, the SUV symbolizes greed, selfishness, and a wish to consort with terrorists. What nonsense!

The critics conveniently ignore the fact that SUVs come in a variety of sizes, many of which use less fuel than full-size sedans or American-as-apple-pie minivans, which, for reasons beyond my powers of analysis, have avoided the wrath of the virtuous.

Depending on which figures you use, there are between 73 and 148 models of SUV to choose from, with new ones rolling off the assembly line every day. They range in price from just under $15,000 for a cute little Japanese model with a tire on the back, to the $105,000 Hummer H1 and his little brother, H2, which are used primarily to attract attention. The less said about them the better.

Regardless of the stridency of the debate, no one could objectively deny that SUVs are practical. Can you remember when stores actually delivered anything other than major appliances to your home? When was the last time you had a television set delivered? Before we had our little truck, the last few "big-box" items we bought had to be wedged into the trunk of our car, with the lid secured by a rope. That really looked cool – our luxury sedan tied shut with a rope.

At an office supply store, the display model was the only one left of my preferred desk chair. No way would it have fit in the back of our car. But it slipped into the SUV with room to spare, sparing us the agony of assembling it ourselves.

As my mother has aged, it has become more difficult to get her into and out of a car. We used to lower her into our car, fearing that we might need a winch to lift her back out, cracking bones along the way. Now, she just swings her lower half into the SUV – the seats are at fanny level – and puts her little feet right down on the sidewalk to get out.

I'm not planning any off-road expeditions in the near future, but the fact that my SUV has all-wheel drive means that, for the first time in the nine years we've lived on our mini-mountain, I haven't gotten stuck in the snow halfway up the hill or had to call AAA to rescue me from my own driveway.

Progress is not always agreeable and, as Jane Ace of *Easy Aces* said, "You've got to take the bitter with the better." Like cell phones, which, in the wrong hands are a blight on civil society, SUVs driven by aggressive, inconsiderate boobs can be a menace. But the convenience they offer the average driver makes it a pretty sure thing that they'll be with us for a while.

10

Hold Your Fire!

On a recent Friday night at Heinz Hall, home of the Pittsburgh Symphony, we on stage and in the audience experienced something I cannot remember ever experiencing in my many years of performing with an orchestra. It was at the end of the hour-long "Manfred" Symphony by Tchaikovsky. As a rule, symphony concerts end with ear-splitting fortissimos that are thrilling to the audience and often bring them to their feet in standing ovations. "Daphnis and Chloe," "Pictures at an Exhibition," and the "Firebird" are among those powerful blockbusters.

But occasionally a concluding work ends quietly. And I've wondered if some in the audience feel they haven't gotten their money's worth when they're deprived an ear-shattering fusillade of timpani rolls and cymbal crashes at the finish.

There are a few popular works that end quietly. "Also Sprach Zarathustra," the *2001: A Space Odyssey* music, is an example. Less well-known among works that end quietly is the "Manfred" symphony by Tchaikovsky. When such a piece is played, one hopes that the listeners will savor the atmosphere created by the subdued ending. Such was the case on Friday night at the conclusion of

Maestro Valery Gergiev's reading of the magnificent work.

While not everyone might have agreed with Gergiev's interpretation or technical idiosyncrasies, the ending was magical. Following a final pizzicato, the maestro stood motionless, hands above the score. It was an eloquent silence, which prolonged the solemnity of the moment, letting it fade away like a retreating star. From the stage, I heard no sound – not a cough, not the rattle of a program – nothing. The silence seemed to last forever, and it was spellbinding, a profound experience often wished for but seldom realized. Three thousand souls sat motionless, their deliverance from the mundane prolonged for another few seconds.

But on Sunday afternoon, it was a different story. The smattering of applause after the first movement did not bode well for the finale of the work. And my forebodings were right. The maestro had barely indicated the final, pianissimo pizzicato when someone yelled "BRAVO!" at the top of his lungs. While it might have been gratifying to know that the gentleman enjoyed "Manfred," I would like him to know that his exuberance shattered the mood, broke the tension, and deprived the rest of us a repeat of Friday evening's wondrous moment.

There has been much debate about applause at symphony orchestra concerts, when a work has multiple sections or movements. Some think it is outdated to expect listeners to hold their applause until the end, and that they should be able to express their jubilation between movements if so inclined. If that's the case, why not just applaud or shout out *during* the movements, whenever the spirit moves you? Rock concert fans do it all the time.

But symphonies and other classical works with multiple sections have continuity for a reason. Although they are performed in segments, they constitute a *whole* and should be appreciated as such.

Applause in between movements fractures the mood and, on occasion, rattles the performers. Instead of concentrating on the music, the performer has to decide whether to acknowledge the applause politely, thus encouraging it, or ignore it, hoping the violators will get the message. Violators *seldom* get the message. "Who, *me?*"

Perhaps the gentleman who shouted out after "Manfred" wanted all of us to know that he, more than anyone else in the hall, knew that the piece was over. But I would like to suggest that he and others who are guilty of jumping the gun, to get a grip on themselves and *wait* until the time is right. When is that? Trust me – you will know. You will know from what is happening on the stage. When the musicians lower their instruments, when the conductor lowers his baton, you *will* know.

11

Jack Ryan Doesn't Get It

Jack Ryan, a Republican from the state of Illinois, was forced to withdraw from the 2004 United States Senate race due to an alleged sex scandal involving his relationship with his ex-wife, actress Jeri Ryan. His eventual replacement, Alan Keyes, would go on to lose the general election to State Senator and future President of the United States, Barack Obama.

Jack Ryan is incapable of understanding that he has done something of which he should be ashamed. Ryan is the Illinois Republican businessman who was running for the U.S. Senate until somehow his divorce documents got opened. In them, his ex-wife alleges that Ryan took her to sex clubs in this country and abroad, where he tried to induce her to have sex with him while others watched. Whoever told him that this would be a "two-day story" must have been living in another universe for the past few decades. In this universe we wring the slightest trace of grit and grime out of stories like this one until the last trace of sediment is sucked down the drain.

Ryan seems to think he deserves to be congratulated because he didn't cheat on his wife. After all, his unseemly behavior was perpetrated within the bounds of matrimony. Well, golly gee – somebody please find a gold star to put on this man's forehead! I sat in front of my television, mouth agape, as Ryan told ABC's John Stossel, "I think we need more people going to Washington who want to engage in marital relations with their wives. I think that's a good thing for this country, not a bad thing." Is this guy clueless or what?

What is it with some of his generation, the baby boomers who have taken it upon themselves to demolish long-established standards of decorum? Why is the concept of shame so foreign to them? Why are they incapable of being embarrassed or admitting any wrongdoing? And what ever happened to personal responsibility? What ever happened to, "I was wrong" or "I made a mistake"? Seems simple enough and quite admirable to admit. But Ryan sees himself as a victim. The fault rests with everyone but him – the judge who opened the court documents, the media, his ex-wife, the astonished public.

Ryan asks, with a trace of exasperation, "What benefit has the public now derived from knowing this information? There is no allegation of breaking any laws, no allegation of infidelity, no allegation of breaking any marriage vows."

Well, since you asked, Mr. Ryan, I'll tell you what benefit the public has derived from knowing this since you seem to be so unaware of how people are supposed to conduct themselves: The public now knows that you are a person of questionable moral judgment who is incapable of distinguishing repugnant behavior from the behavior of the normal people who go about their daily lives without visiting sex clubs and without exposing their kinky turn-ons to others.

The public now knows that you are willing to justify, with a straight face, anything you might want to do by the use of twisted, self-serving logic. It's true – you didn't break any laws. There are a great many acts that can be performed by humans, which are distasteful, and not against civil law, but that are certainly against the civilized laws of polite society. Scratching your rear end is not against the law, but nice people do not do it in public.

You spoke to the national television audience, with that ten-year-old schoolboy grin, as if you just couldn't understand why we think you're a jerk. You said your primary concern about the opening of the documents was that you wanted to keep the information from your young son. When he found out you were quitting your campaign, he was stunned, although he didn't know the reason. Have you told him yet?

I doubt that you have, because I don't think you really understand why yourself. It's a shame that you missed the boat somewhere along the line. You are behaviorally challenged, Mr. Ryan, because you never learned good judgment and the ability to discern normal behavior from aberrant behavior. I'm glad you've dropped out of the race because I wouldn't want to have someone who can't tell the difference making laws that I have to follow.

My long-gone father, who was born near the end of the nineteenth century, used a term that I have thought of many times as I scratch my head in amazement at what has become acceptable in our society. He spoke about "the fitness of things," which is a way – old-fashioned and probably incomprehensible to you, Mr. Ryan – of determining the rightness or wrongness of one's actions. Right? Wrong? Huh?

Back in those days, people *knew* what *fit* behavior was. It was pretty clear-cut before we rationalized our way into the age of moral relativism.

We are all sinners. But some of us remain who recognize our transgressions and try in some way to atone for them. We feel contrite. We acknowledge our lapses of character and try to do better. But you wouldn't know about that, Mr. Ryan, since you are simply a victim.

If you wanted to use this experience for good you could use it as a lesson to your son. You would take him aside and tell him that you dropped out of the Senate race because you had exercised poor judgment. You didn't do anything illegal, something you could be put in jail for, but something that self-respecting people don't do.

And you would tell him that you decided to punish *yourself* by leaving the campaign. What a positive example that would set. But that level of personal accountability would require a measure of character that I'm afraid you, Jack Ryan, do not possess.

PART II
2008-2013

2008

1

What Was He Thinking?

Not a day goes by that there isn't something in the news that has me wondering, à la the late late-night television talk host Tom Snyder, "What were they THINKING?"

And I wondered the same thing when I heard about morning talk host Don Imus's latest utterance. As if he hadn't already gotten himself into hot water last year over his "nappy-headed ho's" remark about the Rutgers women's basketball team, he's gone and done it again. Regardless of his explanation for asking an on-air cohort the race of oft-arrested Dallas Cowboys cornerback Adam Jones, who is African-American, it was stupid of him to respond, "There you go. Now we know."

Imus can't be completely stupid, so why has he made yet another incendiary statement? He couldn't need publicity that badly. And, having dodged a bullet last year, one would think he might have learned some kind of lesson.

Does he really think that, because he hired several African-American assistants after last year's gaffe, he is justified in blurting out whatever thoughts pop into his brain? Does he really think that hiring several African-American assistants after last year's gaffe justifies

43

expressing whatever controversial thoughts pop into his brain?

He asked, "How insane would I have to be? What would I be thinking?" I have to wonder the same thing.

We live in the age of the sound bite, where one or two words, taken out of context, become the whole story. Think of the Reverend Jeremiah Wright whose intemperate ravings were boiled down to their most sulfurous elements and broadcast on a never-ending loop until we all cried for mercy. Context be damned.

Mr. Imus had better learn to err on the side of caution. He's already dodged a couple of bullets, and in his game of Russian roulette it won't be long before he blows his head off.

2

Three Cheers for Trader Joe's

I've *been* shopping at Trader Joe's in East Liberty. It's not exactly a hop, skip and a jump from our house in the western suburbs, but because I've been going to a trainer in that part of town, I can easily pop over to TJ's and, if necessary, put my purchases in the freezer at the training facility, where they keep the ice packs.

We recently invited a neighborhood couple over to try some of our Trader Joe's favorites. I have never before considered serving a frozen entrée to company. But I'm getting to the stage where any assistance, in the kitchen or elsewhere, is appreciated. TJ's carries a couple of delicious entrées that, as the package says, are good enough to serve to company. The one we chose for that evening was Salmon Mojito. I served it with Basmati rice, steamed asparagus with sesame seeds, and French rolls, which, although despite the Trader Joe's package label, we know are made by Mediterra, a nearby specialty bakery that supplies restaurants and supermarkets.

For dessert I had planned to serve Rita's fabulous raspberry sorbet. But word must have gotten around, because the freezer space at TJ's where the raspberry should have been was a yawning void. But I caught sight of another flavor that expunged raspberry from my mind – Double Rainbow Mango Tangerine. Woo-hoo! That more than made up for the missing raspberry.

I had already bought blueberries and raspberries at a good price at, of all places, Whole Foods, where they were selling that day for a respectable $2.99 a carton. I wondered for two seconds how they would look in a goblet with mango sorbet and decided that they would look just fine. And they did, served with a plate of Trader Joe's dark chocolate Florentine lace cookies. You absolutely cannot eat just one.

Appetizers included a delicious but overly crumbly Stilton, a red pepper hummus, and Calbee Snapea Crisps. My husband Charlie and I had first tasted those crunchy delights in Phoenix. I couldn't get enough of them, and our guests felt the same way. But beware! Although the package informs us that they are baked, they are *not* a diet food. One ounce contains 150 calories. Try them anyway.

If you've never been to a Trader Joe's, get yourself to one as soon as possible. You will be cheered by the interesting-looking people who work and shop there and by the astonishing variety of unusual and delicious things for sale. And you will be even more cheered by the total on your register receipt.

And I swear – Trader Joe did not pay me one red cent to write any of the above.

3

Waste

I throw away too much food. Sometimes it's because of unwise choices at the supermarket. Why else would I purchase a pound of turkey bacon *and* a pound of low-fat hot dogs at the same time? Both contain a considerable amount of sodium, so my husband Charlie, who has high blood pressure, won't be eating much of either. I suppose I could have frozen both, but the hot dogs turned out to be so lacking in real hot dog flavor that I decided to consign the last few to the black hole in the kitchen sink. The bacon is still in the fridge, but I bought it last Monday, so the only thing to do with it now is to pitch it. Yes, I should have frozen it. Although regular bacon doesn't always react well to freezing, perhaps turkey bacon would do better in the freezer.

Sometimes I throw away food because I have to buy way more of it than I need. My produce drawer is where parsley, celery, and cilantro go to die – or to put it more graphically – turn to fuzzy goop. Limes, much more so than lemons, go bad quickly. And I'm still waiting to *need* an entire package of fresh rosemary. I could dry leftover fresh herbs, but if that's the case why not just buy the dried version to begin with? I recently promised myself not to waste money on fresh parsley any more.

It seems foolish to buy a bunch of parsley when hardly any recipe calls for more than a few tablespoons. I wonder, when I tackle that new crab cake recipe today, how it will turn out if I use dried parsley. Will my husband know the difference? Would you?

What about a group of neighbors forming a produce-sharing cooperative? Buy a bunch of any of the items mentioned above, divide it into three or four portions, and give it to your neighbors. And they could reciprocate.

When we were children we were told to eat everything on our plates because there are many children in the world, who are not as fortunate as you are, who go to bed hungry. We were taught that it was sinful to throw food away. But we've become pretty cavalier about dumping food into the garbage disposal. Perhaps, with conservation becoming more important each day, we can think of better ways to use our surplus food.

There are a lot of people in this world who don't have enough to eat, many of them right here in Pittsburgh. It's too bad that we can't take all of those leftover herbs, celery, cilantro and parsley to the Food Bank.

4

Technical Support

I ordered a new computer yesterday. As you know, a computer purchased more than two years ago might as well have been purchased in 1917. My Dell has been limping along for three-quarters of a decade with Windows 2000. Obsolescence, thy name is hard drive. The 1917 bit is an exaggeration, but I've been getting messages telling me that my old dinosaur will not accept this program or that download. "Windows 2000? Surely you jest!"

A couple of weeks ago my Outlook Express Inbox mail started disappearing – after I had read it – if I went to any other folder. This was puzzling, and I had to come up with clever ways to save anything important. I stashed most of it in the Deleted Mail folder. And I asked my correspondents to e-mail me simultaneously at my Hotmail account, in case what they sent to Outlook went missing.

After deciding that a virus was eating my email, I contacted Dell's technical support. You know by now that none of these people wants to talk to you. They will do anything they can – throw broken glass under your tires, put up detour signs, tie your ankles together – ANYTHING, to keep you from getting to a real person.

They encourage you to "visit" their online site. They suggest that you go to their list of Frequently Asked Questions. (I'd like to suggest what they can do with their FAQ's.)

To prevent you from conversing with a real person, they have developed a means by which you can "dialogue" with a real person, onscreen. A little dialogue box appears. The support person introduces himself: "Hello, my name is Raj. May I call you Patricia?" Click. I write back, "Call me Pat." Click. "OK, Pat." Click. We're friends now. I type out my problem – click! Then Raj types out an answer – click! And back and forth it goes like that for maybe half an hour. Wouldn't things go faster if Raj and I could just *talk* to each other using our *actual voices?*

The Outlook Express problem was not solved by Raj or his buddy Luciano over at Microsoft.

My last resort was my Internet Service Provider, Comcast. This fellow, a *real person*, who spoke English without an accent, suggested that I go to the Outlook Express dropdown menus, click on "View," then "Current View." Once there, I found several choices (which, of course, have been there since 2000) including "Hide Read Messages" and "Show All Messages." I clicked on "Show All Messages" and poof! There before my eyes was all of my Inbox mail, going back to March. It wasn't a bug. It wasn't obsolescence. It was stupidity. Mine. The solution was at my fingertips the entire time.

But I do wonder a couple of things: Why didn't either the Dell or the Microsoft techie ask me if I had explored the "View" menu? Probably because it didn't occur to them that the person they were talking to was so stupid that she hadn't already done so. They didn't know this person.

I also wonder – although it's obviously possible to do – why anyone would *want* to hide their read messages.

All along I suspected that my email disappeared because of something I had done. But I didn't know what I had done or how to undo it. The Comcast fellow said that this kind of thing happens when one accidentally performs a Keyboard Shortcut.

So, before you waste a lot of valuable time developing a relationship with Technical Support, make sure you've explored all of the possibilities that are right in front of your face. My "complicated" problem was solved with exactly three clicks of a mouse.

The doorbell just rang. It's my new computer!

5

Things Gathering Dust

Before he was unceremoniously dumped from Pittsburgh's air waves, popular Pittsburgh talk radio host Doug Hoerth treated his listeners to daily readings from Rosie O'Donnell's blog. He introduced these entries with a sappy French chanson and read them in a wispy, feminine voice. Rosie's blog is what most would agree is "mindless drivel." I think she sees her musings as the twenty-first century's answer to haiku. A sample:

> blake and i fishing
> jumpin in the hudson
> clean now
> it's ok

I won't give you a link to her web site although you're perfectly welcome to venture there on your own.

I hope that my writings are not mindless drivel, although I may be drifting in that direction even as I write this.

The last few days have been taken up with the laying of new carpet in four rooms, beginning with the dining area. It's nearly the same color as the old carpet – sort of a dark teal – so I'll have to put up a sign with a big arrow pointing down that reads, "New carpet."

While moving tons of stuff back into my recarpeted office I discovered some interesting items. My husband and I went through the contents of a letter holder that has seen many seasons come and go, unattended, on top of a bookcase.

There are wonderfully kind notes and letters – some from people who are no longer with us – and the funeral program of my beautiful Westinghouse High School and Carnegie Tech friend June Harris, who was buried in September 2002, at the age of 61. She played the cello. She was one of five. Her oldest sister died less than two months later. Their poor mother.

There are congratulatory notes following performances, including one from Natasha Snitkovsky, the woman I consider Pittsburgh's finest pianist. I appreciate those warm expressions even more in retrospect than I did when they arrived.

There's a paper facsimile of Mr. Squiggly. Mr. Squiggly is a round-headed yellow timer with flexible arms and legs, a suction cup under his butt and a magnet on his back. So you can plant him just about anywhere. I took along one of his clones as a dinner gift. The recipient designed a paper facsimile and included it with a thank you note.

There's a bumper sticker that reads, "The Symphony Is for You!" It wasn't a Pittsburgh Symphony sticker. I had brought a bunch of them back from San Antonio when I had played the "Rhapsody in Blue" with their

orchestra, thinking that somebody at the Pittsburgh
Symphony might like to create an equally catchy bumper sticker. They never did. The suggestion would have
had to come from a better salesperson than I.

There's a spot-on cartoon of former PSO manager
Gideon Toeplitz displaying the linings of his empty
pockets to demonstrate that there's no money for orchestra raises. It's one of dozens created by PSO violist
Isaias Zelkowicz who is a cartooning genius. He has lam-
pooned a *Who's Who* of conductors and other musical
figures much to the delight of his fellow musicians. He
could make a living delighting a bigger audience. But
he'd rather play the viola.

There's a Garfield card, sent to Heinz Hall in 1987,
with the printed message: "If I had to choose between
eating, sleeping and thinking of you...you'd definitely
finish on top!" This fellow had become smitten with me
at, of all places, Benkovitz Seafoods in the Strip District.
Included in the card was a flattering handwritten note –
I'll spare you – and his business card as Secretary
Treasurer of a Teamsters local. I didn't respond to his
message although including his business card was evidently an invitation to do so.

There's an editorial from *The Philadelphia Inquirer*
of March 13, 1980, which reads, in part: "Sam Evans,
explaining his opposition to the senatorial candidacy
of state representative Joseph Rhodes Jr., recently told
reporters that he was against Mr. Rhodes because Mr.
Rhodes was not black enough. That's incredible."

Joe Rhodes is the product of an Asian mother and a black father. I wonder if Sam Evans is still around. If he is, he must be watching the presidential race with a good bit of interest if not downright consternation.

6

The Ladies Who Lunch

Until yesterday, my friend Jean, who lives in Washington County, had never been to Whole Foods or to Pittsburgh's wine-deprived version of Trader Joe's. (In Pennsylvania liquor is sold only in state-owned Wine and Spirits stores.) She had also never been to the restaurant Casbah on Highland Avenue between East Liberty and Shadyside. For non-Pittsburghers reading this, Casbah is a member of the eclectic Big Burrito Group. Its cuisine is described as Mediterranean-North African. Others in the group are Soba (Pan Asian), Umi (Japanese) Kaya (Caribbean), Eleven (upscale contemporary), and Mad Mex (Mexican) of which there are six, including one at Penn State and one in Philadelphia.

When Jean and I decided to launch an attack on East Liberty/Shadyside, Casbah was the first stop. There was a parking space right in front of the door. (Was "The Secret" at work?)

Jean loved Casbah. She loved the atmosphere. She loved the menu. She loved the crisp white tablecloths. And she *loved* the wine flights. Casbah is one of few local restaurants that offer you your own mini wine tasting at a reasonable price. A flight consists of three different wines, from groups with such whimsical appellations as "The

Chardonnay Buffet," or "No Country for Old Wine," or "Land Down Under." Jean chose "The Sparkler" and I ordered the "Chardonnay Buffet." The three glasses are placed on a sheet of paper with the name of each wine in a circle, in case you want to jot it down and try (I said *try*) to find it in a Pennsylvania state store. And I really believe that for ten to twelve dollars you get more wine than if you had ordered a single glass, some of which are the same price as the flights.

We split an arugula salad with crimini mushrooms, pancetta, potatoes and Capriole goat cheese. This is not, I repeat *not*, a low calorie salad – but it is divine and worth skimping on dinner.

They let us split an order of sea scallops with red pepper casareccia – a pasta we had never heard of – and jumbo lump crabmeat. It was luscious, and a half-order was perfect for one. Not many humans that I can think of would be justified in eating an entire order of this rich dish for lunch.

This delightful meal, wine flights and all, cost us thirty dollars apiece, including the tip. (We got a grip on ourselves and did not order dessert.) We spend nearly as much at Houlihan's and the Olive Garden. And there's no comparison.

The service was pleasant, although there is an African-American barmaid/waitress who has worked there for years, who is a little too cool for my money. I've dined in that place so many times she has to recognize me. How nice it would be if she greeted me with something like, "Good to see you." Nothing extravagant, just ordinary *pleasantness*. But she just isn't friendly. Maybe being friendly isn't cool. And Casbah is nothing if not cool.

Neither Jean nor I bought much at Whole Foods. When you know you're on your way to Trader Joe's, Whole Foods is merely a "courtesy" stop.

We managed to find plenty at TJ's. I kept taking items to Jean's basket saying, "Buy it, you'll like it." Two of the items were the Calbee Snapea Crisps and the dark chocolate-coated Florentine lace cookies that I served company last Friday.

She emailed me later: "Snacks made out of peas. Of course I HAD to try them. Another winner. I thought, 'Well, I learned something else at Trader Joe's. This was the best thing I bought today'. Wrong. I then tried one of the lace cookies – or rather the thick chunks of wonderful dark chocolate (it's a health food, you know) covered with a 'smidgeon' of crushed almond cookie. I immediately put them in the freezer. Only ate the broken ones; no calories in those. I hope they aren't still around when I am depressed, happy, hungry, a bit hungry, not really hungry, bored, or well, basically still breathing. Boy, are they good. I am totally passing up dinner."

So there you have it. What could be more fun than two friends enjoying a delightful afternoon of dining and shopping? And, to top it off, the weather was gorgeous.

7

Working the Phones

Although I seem to get a lot done, I'm fundamentally a lazy person. Much of what I do I wouldn't do if someone else would do it for me. I would just as soon spend my entire day sitting at this keyboard or the one with eighty-eight black and white keys. For variety, I get up now and then to engage in a little eating and shopping. But exert myself? Only when unavoidable. All of those closets that were going to be cleaned out and organized when I retired? They are still awaiting their new life.

But the extraordinary nature of this presidential campaign has stoked my energy and spirited me off to toil in the trenches of a nearby Obama "Campaign for Change" office. And it lifts my spirits to think that I am a little wave in this tsunami of support for the brilliant young man who might later tonight be elected our next president.

If anyone had told me, even six months ago, that clusters of *white* people, young and old, would be streaming into an office in that particular upscale community – or any community, for that matter – to work on behalf of an African-American presidential candidate, I would have considered him or her delusional. But I started noticing Obama signs in yards in unexpected places. And I began to think there might be hope.

And now, hundreds of volunteers have made their way to Pittsburgh from all over the country, some at considerable financial and professional sacrifice, to help push this battle-ground state over the top and into the Obama camp.

Here they have been, day in and day out, working the phones and laptops, tallying the numbers, cranking out lists of phone numbers and talking points for those of us who wandered in off the street willing to sit down for a couple of hours to face the uncertainty of calling complete strangers. We were pleasantly engaged by a few and hung up on by a few. But we mostly listened to the robotic voices of answering machines. When *are* people at home?

There hasn't been much time, during this flurry of activity, to reflect upon how truly significant all of this is. But I think about how wonderful it would be if all of those back in time, who worked so hard and even risked their lives so that others might VOTE, could witness what an extraordinary event is taking place.

Barack Obama's run for the presidency hasn't happened out of a clear blue sky. Many small steps prepared us for this day. Edward Brooke became the first African-American senator. Carl Stokes became the first African-American mayor of a major city, Cleveland, Ohio. Doug Wilder became the first African-American governor of a state, Virginia. They were followed, either through election or appointment, by a widening circle of black mayors, cabinet officers, and other public officials. And no matter how fed up we might have become with George Bush and the devastation he and his cohort wreaked upon this country during the last eight years, he deserves credit for one thing: In his selection of Colin Powell and Condoleezza Rice as his secretaries of state, he helped the country get used to seeing African Americans in the highest decision-making roles.

Unless something unexpected happens between now and tomorrow evening, we will know who our next president is by early Wednesday morning. Regardless of how it turns out, there is no adequate way to thank all of those determined souls, some of whom put in hundred-hour weeks and existed on very little food, to get their candidate, *my* candidate, elected. We have broken through an important barrier we won't be revisiting.

That isn't to say that racism will be behind us. Anyone who believes that is a dreamer. But in this effort to elect Barack Obama there has been a commingling of people with a common purpose that has brought together those who might never have stumbled upon one another for any other reason. We know, more than ever, that we share more similarities than differences. And our sense of purpose and our humanity have been enhanced.

8

This was published in the Pittsburgh Post-Gazette *on the Monday after the election of Barack Obama to the presidency.*

November 6, 2008

My Flag

I dashed into the neighborhood party supply store the morning after the election of Barack Obama and bought every American flag pin in stock – twenty-two in all. I decided to lay in a good supply and give one to each of my Obama-supporter friends.

The flag was an issue in the presidential campaign. A big deal was made of the fact that Barack Obama wasn't wearing a flag pin at one of the debates. This was just one of an endless list of nit-picky things thrown at him during the campaign to try to make him seem unfit for the highest office in the land. He couldn't possibly be a real American.

Somewhere along the line the American flag was hijacked by an element of American society that decided that if one didn't display a flag on one's lapel or in one's yard, if one didn't fly Old Glory from his pickup truck, or loudly sing "The Star Spangled Banner" at baseball games, one wasn't a real American.

What *is* a real American? For African Americans the flag and other symbols of patriotism have always been problematical. Yes, we are citizens of this country. We pay taxes, and we grill hot dogs on the Fourth of July and Memorial Day – those holidays on which I dig out our little flag and stick it in the ground out front, near the mailbox. It seems like the right thing to do, sort of. But I always feel a wee bit sheepish, as if I'm treading on territory where I'm not sure I'm welcome, the way I might feel if I wandered into a NASCAR rally.

Because the full rights of citizenship were so grudgingly bestowed upon the descendants of African slaves, is it any wonder that we might not be chest-thumping patriots – even though we have fought and died for this country in many wars?

My mother used to accuse my father of being "deliberately obtuse" on certain issues, and there is much to suggest that a lot of white people are deliberately obtuse about our less-than-effusive patriotism. And there's a Catch 22 element to the position in which we find ourselves. We're reminded in many subtle ways that we're less than welcome in this country, and then we're accused of not being patriotic. Hey guys: You can't have it both ways.

Just think: We live in a country where, in the last century, there were many places where Barack Obama, because of his brown skin, would have had to step off the curb to let a white person pass. When your people have been treated that way, something hard to eradicate insinuates itself into your DNA.

On "The View" the morning after the election, Whoopi Goldberg said that her reaction to Obama's victory was that maybe she could finally put down her suitcase. I know just how she feels. Despite the many blessings that have been bestowed on her in this country, she has never quite felt welcome here. That's a concept that's impossible for anybody who hasn't experienced it to grasp.

I bought the flag pins, and I will wear one of them proudly, because the election of Barack Obama, with the help of millions of fellow citizens of good will, makes me feel as if maybe I really do belong here, and that the United States of America has at last earned my willingness to call myself a patriot.

2009

9

January 2009

Topping Off My Brain

Auto racing? Spare me. No interest. Zero. Nada. That sport – *is* it a sport? – has never appealed to me in any way. It has always been one of those things that, if I ignored it or pretended it wasn't there, would quietly – or come to think of it – noisily go away. I know the names Earnhart, Andretti, and Petty, and I know there's a hot-looking babe who races cars named Danica Patrick. I hope she wins, although I doubt if I'll be watching.

A few weeks ago my friend Susie, whose reading tastes I know nothing about, recommended a book titled *The Art of Racing in the Rain* by Garth Stein. Other than recommending it, the only clue she gave about its contents was that the story is told by a dog. Well, I like dogs, and I like things that are offbeat, so the book sounded like it would be right up my alley.

I gave little thought to what the title, *The Art of Racing in the Rain,* might mean. Susie had recommended it, which was the only endorsement I needed. If I thought about it at all, I simply figured that the dog must be telling us about dog-like activities such as chasing cars in the rain.

That did not turn out to be the case. In this beautifully written novel about love, loss and triumph, the dog, Enzo, is a Golden Retriever whose master is a professional race car driver. Enzo shares with the reader tidbits of the special knowledge a race car driver must have in order to win – or at least not kill himself – in all sorts of hazardous situations, especially on wet pavement. I'm glad I didn't know all that ahead of time because I probably wouldn't have bought the book.

Last Sunday morning, as I scanned the radio dial for something that wasn't an infomercial or a dry-as-dust public service program, I stumbled upon a sports station. The subject was auto racing, and until a week ago I would have changed the dial faster than a speeding bullet. But I listened for a few minutes as the hosts expounded on things that sounded familiar – corners and back straight, hot laps and limits of adhesion. Hoo-eee!

I don't expect to be tossing those terms around at the next cocktail party. But even at my slightly advanced age, small talk isn't the only reason to learn new things. How about expanding one's knowledge?

My brain has the capacity to hold only so much information. As it is, I've lately been leaking some of its contents like the ice man's truck on a summer day. That becomes clearer every evening during "Jeopardy." But leak as it might, the old crankcase between my ears still seems willing to tuck in a few new nuggets of knowledge now and then. That gives me hope that, in its "as these retire let others follow" mode, it will continue to make room for fresh knowledge right up to the "full" line.

If someone had asked me two weeks ago if I knew anything about auto racing, I would have answered,

"You've got to be kidding." But I know a little now – enough to realize that auto racing isn't a complete waste of time.

If you're looking for something mind-expanding to read during these cold winter nights, something vastly different from what you're reading now, I recommend *Consider the Lobster* by David Foster Wallace, author of the acclaimed 1996 novel *Infinte Jest,* one of *Time* magazine's 100 Best English-language Novels from 1923 to 2005. Unfortunately for his fans, Wallace decided to hang himself last September.

Consider the Lobster is a collection of essays written for publications such as *Gourmet, Rolling Stone, Harper's,* and *The Atlantic Monthly.* Wallace's subjects are all over the place; there's bound to be at least one that will appeal to you. Whether it's about his visit to the 2003 Maine Lobster Festival, John McCain's 2000 presidential run, the porn film industry, or a discussion of the battle between English-usage prescriptivists and descriptivists, you will not be bored by Wallace's unconventional way of viewing the world or his voluminous use of footnotes, asides, exegeses, and digressions. His style takes a little getting used to, but if you manage to get on board, you'll probably enjoy the ride. One doesn't just *read* Wallace; one *experiences* Wallace.

10

Sports and the Men in My Life

My father was a baseball fan. He was fifty-three in 1947 when Jackie Robinson was signed by the Brooklyn Dodgers, and believe me, that day was as exciting to him in 1947 as Barack Obama's election to the presidency was to me in 2008.

My father and I weren't especially close. After work he often attended board meetings, and his newspaper job frequently took him out of town, even out of the country. In his absence, my mother and I had plenty of projects to keep us busy. She taught me how to knit and embroider. She taught me how to cook. When I was twelve, she taught me how to type, a skill that I value more each day as I go like the wind at my electronic keyboard while others, who weren't so fortunate, continue to hunt and peck with two fingers.

In my late teens, I decided that learning about baseball would give me something to share with my father. I started listening to Bob Prince describing the Pittsburgh Pirates games on the radio and enjoyed it more each day as my understanding increased. I memorized the names and numbers of the players and the requirements of each position and, as you can imagine, my father was thrilled to have a buddy with whom he could share his love of the game.

Until the election of Barack Obama, the most joyous day of my adulthood was October 13, 1960, when Bill Mazeroski hit a home run in the bottom of the 9th, with the score tied 9 to 9, to win the World Series for the underdog Pittsburgh Pirates, who had been outscored by the New York Yankees 55-27 in the Series. And as I write this, nearly five decades later, my eyes grow moist as I relive that wonderful day.

It's too bad that the Pittsburgh Pirates have since plummeted from the top of the heap to the bottom. New stadium notwithstanding, it is a source of extreme puzzlement to me why people still go to their games.

My husband is a football fan. For a few years, when he talked to me about what was happening in whatever game he was watching, I would remain mute for fear that, if I showed the slightest interest, I would be peppered with football minutia every Sunday for the next five months. I didn't want to come right out and say, "I really don't give a hoot," but that's what I was thinking.

Then one day it occurred to me that millions of women would sell their souls to have a nice husband to enjoy *anything* with, a football game, a tractor pull, *anything*. But there sat my spouse, alone in our den, sharing his joys and frustrations with the walls and the TV screen.

So I bought myself a copy of Joe Theismann's *Football for Dummies* and read a little of it. But I learned more simply by watching the games and asking questions. It took a while, and I would forget much of what I had learned from one season to the next. However, one day a light bulb went on over my head and I, at long last, understood the *downs*. After that rather simple concept sank in, other aspects of the game fell into place. There's still much I don't understand. But I know enough to enjoy the game, although it was a long time before I could watch the players crashing to the ground or into each other without flinching. I realize that it's a contact sport, and the players know going in that their bodies are going to take a beating.

Until the late 1950s, baseball was *the* American sport. Then along came the Super Bowl and baseball receded into the shadows. Enthusiasm for football is nowhere more evident than among Steelers fans. In the January 26th issue of *Newsweek*, Pittsburgh native Howard Fineman, in an article titled "Our New Tribes," writes: "They call themselves a 'nation' and gather in the fall or early winter, usually on Sundays. The faithful wear clothing emblazoned with the names of their heroes; they pray by twirling a sacred talisman, a black-and-gold terry-cloth hand towel, at times achieving dervish-like ecstasy. They are the hundreds of Pittsburgh Steelers fans, cheering at ear-splitting volume, in a crowd composed of myriad races, ethnicities and hometowns, many far beyond western Pennsylvania...'Steeler Nation' is one of the planet's most populous and intense sports-fan cohorts." The members of this new tribe have little in common aside from their fanatical love of the Pittsburgh Steelers.

As I asserted in the previous article, it's never a waste of time to inject new information into the old brain cells. And by learning to enjoy football, I've fired up a few synapses, earned my membership in Steeler Nation and – most important – made my husband happy.

Pittsburgh's going to the Super Bowl! Again!

The Steelers won their sixth Super bowl on February 1, 2009.

11

Old Haunts Revisited

When I was in high school, my girlfriends and I indulged in something nearly every day that was pretty unusual for a group of teenage girls to do. So unusual, in fact, that it's hard for me to believe, looking back, that it's true. Instead of going to band rehearsal or cheer leader practice, we played cards, all kinds of cards, at Carol and Tootsie Velar's house on Chaucer Street, not far from Westinghouse High School. And although I have little memory of how our parents reacted to this somewhat unorthodox daily activity, it's a good bet that they knew we could have been doing something much worse. Most of us were good students – on the honor roll. And Carol and Tootsie's mother was always at home. I have no idea how she felt about our taking over her dining room every day, but she was unfailingly gracious and welcoming.

Our card-playing mini-marathon began with bid whist, a precursor to the game of bridge that is still a favorite in England, among African Americans, and in the U. S. military. Soon we branched out to hearts, canasta and pinochle. And when there weren't enough of us for a four-person game we played gin rummy.

In that environment I didn't become a skilled card player. We didn't sit around analyzing a hand for a half hour after it was over. We would forget the cards as soon as they were played. But we were playing for fun, not blood, so skill was of minimal importance. As long as you were sentient enough to follow suit, you were welcome to sit at the table.

In college I squeezed in hundreds of games of hearts in the dining hall – while corroding my insides with nickel cups of coffee – between long hours of doing what I was supposed to be doing – learning how to play the piano well enough to secure gainful employment in the outside world.

The card playing continued when, during the years that the Pittsburgh Symphony went on cross-country bus tours through forest, field, and desert, I took up with the bridge players. The people at Greyhound turned around two sets of seats in the back of the bus, one for our bridge game, the other for a penny ante poker game.

We bridge players were obsessed. If we didn't have a table, we'd play across an aisle. We played in the orchestra lounge. We played in airports. We played in any location where we could improvise a flat surface.

And then – I stopped playing, for reasons I've forgotten. Maybe I just wore myself out or decided that reading or knitting were more worthwhile pastimes.

Fast forward thirty years.

A few Sundays ago a friend invited me to join her in a bridge game with two other women. I didn't think I'd remember anything about the game, and I told her I would come only if they were desperate. They were. I went. And amazingly, like riding a bicycle, the fundamentals came back in a flash.

However, since that Sunday I have not played bridge sitting at a table in a room with other humans, although I'm looking forward to my next in-room game. Meanwhile I've discovered a fantastic web site called Bridge Base Online where there's a never-ending supply of players and games. It's a wonderful haven for bridge buffs, the resources of which I haven't even begun to explore. So far all I've done is click the button that says, "Help me find a game!" and another that says, "Take me to the first available seat," and presto! – I'm at a "table" with three other players who are often in the middle of a contract. Most of these people are in other countries – Italy, Turkey, Sweden, Canada, Poland. In a game the other night, the entire dialogue in the below-table Chat box was in Spanish.

With Bridge Base Online I don't have to try to remember who has the lead or what trumps are, and it's impossible to renege. The board remembers everything for me, although it does not keep me from making dumb mistakes. However, if I do something stupid and get paired up with a grouch, I can make a hasty exit, go to another game, and leave the grouch to mutter imprecations into cyberspace.

Bridge Base Online means that it is no longer necessary, if one is in the mood to play bridge, to dig out one's list of bridge aficionados and canvass by phone or email until three other players succumb to the promise of wine and cheese – plus a little bridge. And if I can't sleep I can play at 3 a.m. There are always several thousand people playing at BBO at the same time.

Another passion, or interest, I'm trying to retrieve is the French I studied in college, most of which is long forgotten. Charlie and I are going to France this summer, so I thought I'd brush up, and I'm doing so with a course I found on Amazon called "Learn French in Your Car." The language is coming back bit by bit and I haven't yet crashed into a lane of parked cars while trying to imitate the voice in the dashboard: "*Avez vous vu votre voiture?*" – or something like that. In France I doubt if I'll need to say anything more urgent than, "May I please have another cake of soap," to the hotel maid. But it can't hurt to exercise my brain.

Because our lives are so busy, we tend to abandon the pleasures of our youth. We even forget what some of them were. Maybe it's time for us to pick up where we left off. And by jostling that sleeping storehouse of knowledge, perhaps we can surpass our previous level of accomplishment. My current goal is to become *better* than mediocre at bridge, although at this stage that might be too much to hope for. Mediocrity at bridge might be baked into my genes.

Not to worry. If I become discouraged, I can always drop into the old bowling alley...

12

The Ending of an Era

I was a newspaper baby – grew up with printer's ink in my veins. My father was the editor of the *Pittsburgh Courier* during its heyday in the 40s and 50s, when Joe Louis was winning at home and black soldiers were winning overseas but coming home to second-class status.

As a teenager I worked at the *Courier* office in the summertime, filling in for employees who were on vacation. I was all over that building – in the editorial, collection, and advertising departments; at the front reception desk; and – my absolute favorite – operating the switchboard, long before automated voices began treating us to exasperating press-a-number recitals.

Our switchboard was the Real McCoy with its tangle of trunk and extension lines. Being in charge of it was a daunting responsibility, especially first thing Monday morning, when out-of-town reporters and advertising representatives would jam the lines. People from near and far were checking in, and it was up to me to hook them up to the right extension.

"Good Morning, Pittsburgh Courier. May I help you?"

"I'd like to speak to Chet Robinson."

"One moment, plee-uz," I would brightly reply, sometimes having to put a caller, who might be calling from Chicago or Los Angeles, on hold until I could finally say, "Mr. Robinson's line is free now, sir. I'll connect you."

When I was nine or ten my father decided that I should have a *Courier* route, to help me learn the value of money. Every week we would drive around the neighborhood in his big Lincoln, delivering the *Courier* to my list of regular customers. You might think that's pretty funny, but don't laugh. With the money saved from my paper route I made a substantial down payment on my first Steinway piano.

I grew up in the newspaper culture and think of newspapers as natural a part of life as the rising and setting as the sun. Morning coffee? Post-Gazette. Plane flight? Add the New York Times.

So it is with profound sadness that I witness the slow, painful demise of the newspapers we have come to know and depend upon. The *Post-Gazette* is shrinking before our eyes, struggling to keep its head above water despite dwindling revenues – even before the financial downturn – forcing it to condense diverse subjects – travel, entertainment, books – into a single section.

But time marches on. Things change. If that weren't the case we'd still be using tire chains and typewriters. It's time to relinquish our romantic notion of the newspaper office with its looming deadlines, clicking teletype machines, and rumbling presses that are the stuff of legend and classic movies.

The Internet is the most transformational development of the modern era, but it has taken a while for those who toil in the newspaper industry to realize that the heralded arrival of computers on their desks marked the beginning of the end.

Five years from now there might not be any daily newspapers, except for a few narrowly-focused publications such as the *Wall Street Journal*, which seems to be one of the few that isn't hemorrhaging money.

Nothing lasts forever.

13

Around the World on the Silver Screen

If you're fed up with the airlines – and who isn't? – you can travel to exotic places, minus the sore feet, in the comfort of your family room, by way of the films listed below.

My husband and I subscribe to Netflix, which has a surprisingly comprehensive library of the kinds of films we like – offbeat, often foreign gems – which my husband discovers as he combs through various publications.

I'll tell you just a little about each film (with a little help from Netflix) although I like to be surprised when I watch a movie and seldom read reviews, in their entirety, until after I've watched the film. We think these are terrific movies. In fact, we've watched some of them twice. Two are from France, two are from Sweden and, except for the last one, they are listed in alphabetical order:

Denmark:
After the Wedding (2006) - To save the failing orphanage he runs in India, Danish transplant Jacob Petersen returns to his homeland to meet a self-indulgent businessman who has offered a generous donation.

Sweden:

Autumn Sonata (1978) - Ingrid Bergman, in her second to last film, plays a mother and world-famous pianist who forsakes a music career to reconcile with her oldest daughter. Directed by Ingmar Bergman.

Morocco, Japan, Mexico, United States:

Babel (2006) - Brad Pitt and Cate Blanchett become involved in a series of events that unfolds across four countries demonstrating both the necessity and impossibility of human communication. (This was the first time we had seen Brad Pitt in a film. He's *good.*)

France:

The Chorus (2004) - Music teacher Clement Mathieu lands a job at a boys boarding school populated by delinquents and orphans.

Iran:

The Color of Paradise (2000) - An 8-year-old blind boy is nearly abandoned by his widowed father at a school for blind children.*

Poland:

The Decalogue (1987) - Using one of the Ten Commandments as a thematic springboard for each film in this collection, writer-director Krzysztof Kieslowski explores the lives of ordinary people flailing through inner torments, hard decisions and shattering revelations.

Albania:
The Forgiveness of Blood (2011) - An Albanian family caught up in a blood feud. Interesting film, interesting language.*

France:
The Girl From Paris (2001) - Fed up with city life, Sandrine decides to leave Paris and live out her dream of becoming a farmer.

Germany:
Goodbye Lenin! (2003) - In East Germany in 1989, Alex Kerner's mother Christiane falls into a coma just as the Berlin Wall is about to come down. (This is one we watched twice.)

South Korea:
Poetry (2010) – As a poetry-writing class inspires serenely self-possessed grandmother   Mija to open her senses to her suburban surroundings, in rushes an array of unsettling discoveries.*

Vietnam:
The Scent of Green Papaya (1993) - The life of ten-year-old Mui, who is in service as a housemaid in prewar Saigon.

Mongolia:

The Story of the Weeping Camel (2003) - Unique documentary about a camel that rejects her newborn white colt.

South Africa:

Tsotsi (2005) - This Oscar-winning Best Foreign Language film shows that no soul is too far gone to be reformed.

Sweden:

Under the Sun (1998) - Lonely, middle-aged Swedish farmer Olef decides to hire a housekeeper.

Israel:

Ushpizin (2004) - A downtrodden couple finds hope and good fortune – amid unexpected houseguests – in this humorous take on religious Jews living in a modern world.

India:

Water (2005) - After losing her husband to illness, 8-year-old Chuyia is forced to live out her days in a temple for Hindu widows.

United States:

Snowcake (2006) - Sigourney Weaver, Alan Rickman. A British man stranded in Ontario is forced to confront his past when he meets an autistic woman.

Bon voyage and enjoy the trip!

*Although this film was made after the above was written, it's an interesting film that should be included.

14

Julia Lives!

Those clattering, squeaky-hinge sounds you hear are the oven doors of fifty million American cooks checking their Bouef à la Bourguignonne. Julia Child, although reportedly deceased, is back among us, and with a vengeance. Thanks to her exhumation by Nora Ephron in the film *Julie and Julia, Mastering the Art of French Cooking* is once again at the top of *The New York Times'* list of hardcover advice books – I suppose cookbooks *are* considered advice – and it is No. 2 on Amazon's Top 100 list. Julia is also the subject of three additional books on various best-seller lists. Julia has been reincarnated.

How many decades ago did I buy my paperback copy of *Mastering the Art of French Cooking?* We all bought a copy. How much we used it is another question. I can't find mine, so it must have gone into a box destined for Goodwill. My recollection is that Julia's recipes were complicated, and, busy with career pursuits, I put her on the back burner. But a lot of us who might now actually have time to cook are happy that we're being given a second chance, and we're buying up every available copy of that weighty tome at up to forty dollars a pop.

While Julia was delighting us with her skillful, mad-cap approach to *haute cuisine* on *The French Chef* on PBS, our culinary world was beginning to expand with the introduction of nouvelle cuisine, California cuisine, Southwest, Mediterranean, fusion, and heaven knows what other manner of fare. And Julia was tucked away in the archives.

Now I'm feeling a little guilty about abandoning Julia back in the twentieth century and am planning to atone for my sins by revisiting *Mastering the Art of French Cooking* and trying my hand at a few of her specialties.

Amid protests from any Francophiles who might be reading this, Pittsburgh has never been as welcoming to French cuisine as most other cities of comparable size. One has to search for a French restaurant here other than Le Pommier in Southside. I don't know why that is. Even Cincinnati, Ohio, not generally thought of as a culinary hotspot, boasted a Mobil Travel Guide five-star French restaurant, La Maisonette, for fifty-six years, until cash flow problems forced it to close in 2005.

But what the heck? We now live in a shopping mall food court culture. In our food-obsessed society, who cares about the quality of the food? Just bring us more of it. And the cheaper the better. For us *haute cuisine* is how high can they pile the toppings on our pizza?

Maybe Julia has been distressed by this lowering of our culinary standards, and that might be why she's paying us a visit. Millions of would-be cooks who might never have heard of Julia Child until Meryl Streep brought her back to life on the screen are about to learn an entirely new way of thinking about food.

Merci, Meryl. Merci, Julia and – bon appétit!

15

Living in the Best of Times

Yesterday was my 68th birthday. The years are stacking up.

We've been watching Ted Koppel's documentary on the Discovery Channel about China titled *The People's Republic of Capitalism.* In a place where only government officials and the very wealthy owned cars until quite recently, everybody, it seems, is now buying a car. Well, not quite everybody. There are still hundreds of millions of dirt-poor peasants outside of the big cities who barely know what a car is. But the newly affluent in cities are buying twenty-five thousand automobiles a day – a DAY. That's more than nine million a year. And the purchasers, many in their thirties, forties, and fifties, have never driven before. The accident rate is stratospheric and the fatality rate enormous. Pedestrians dart across streets where and when they like with little regard for the tons of steel bearing down on them. What will it be like there in ten years? Thousands of miles of new roads are being built, and you know what that means: an even greater explosion of cars.

Charles Dickens wrote about "the best of times" and "the worst of times." I remarked to my husband the other day that he and I might have lived through the best years of human civilization. Although terrible things have happened during our lifetimes, we know that, as good as life has been for us, there will never be an absence of war and famine and injustice.

After so much progress, it looks as if things might be heading somewhere we'd just as soon not go. Whether we like it or not, China seems on its way to becoming the number one world power, simply because there are so bloody many Chinese. We may be witnessing the beginning of the decline and fall of the West.

And while the Chinese are busy taking our jobs, the Muslims are busy trying to take our lives, by any means necessary. And with massive immigration, what will Europe look like in twenty-five years?

The second half of the twentieth century, my half, was amazing. Think of the social changes and the advances in medicine and technology. My father died in 1980. He got to witness four-fifths of the most astonishing century in the history of mankind. He was born in 1895. Think of what the world was like in 1895. And think of how he would react to the world we live in just twenty-eight years after his death.

He would wonder what these screens are that everyone is huddled in front of, pecking away, hour after hour. And what is this object that so many people, walking around in stores and driving their cars, are pressing to their ears? Nothing that small could be a *telephone.* And you can take *pictures* with them?

It's hard even for me to remember what developments that are now part of everyday life simply didn't exist in 1980. Did we have remote controls for our television sets? Did we have microwave ovens? Were cars yet equipped with Cruise Control? Cordless phones in private homes? Cordless phones *anywhere?* It would seem like magic to him.

What would he make of the fact that we can now sit down at our desks and find information about *anything* within a few seconds? We take for granted being able to insert a document into a machine in our office and have it pop out of a similar machine in someone else's office half-way around the world.

Sometimes I think we're becoming too enamored with our own cleverness, by our ability to make into reality nearly anything we can visualize. Does one really *need* a telephone that takes pictures, or a portable media player (iPod) that holds 20,000 songs?

People used to look at me as if I was out of my head when I suggested that a day will come when we will be able to store an entire winter's worth of energy for our homes in a canister the size of a tennis ball can. As we struggle to figure out alternative sources of fuel, my outlandish notion, or something like it, might become reality.

I am grateful to have lived to see the extraordinary transformation of the world from what it was at the beginning of my life to what it has become. The planet is on course to become a more crowded and hostile place in the next few decades. For those of us here now, these might just be "the best of times."

16

Why Did I Wait So Long?

"She was always impeccably groomed" is not a description that future generations will be reading about me. It's all I can do to smear on a little drug store foundation and lipstick. And for special occasions I manage to apply mascara – what doesn't end up on my blouse or the tip of my nose – to my upper lashes. Can't do the lower ones. Mascara on my lower lashes tends to drift downward so that, before the night is over, I look like a character from *Night of the Living Dead.*

Because I am a pianist, I've resigned myself to having split, unattractive nails, hoping only that people will love me for my sparkling arpeggios and not my sleek, polished nails. Manicures for me are a waste of my money because after a few hours of beating the piano keys into submission, my perfect manicure has begun chipping off in layers. But, ever the optimist, I have one done every once in a while regardless.

On one of those occasions, manicure complete, I decided, on a whim, to treat myself to a *pedicure*, although I had always considered the women seated side-by-side in those throne-like chairs reading magazines pretty self-indulgent.

But have a pedicure I did, and to paraphrase Dr. Phil, it was a "changing day in my life."

My feet were placed in a tub of warm, bubbling blue water, where they were massaged and anointed – all the way up to my knees. Various smoothing and trimming procedures were performed on my grateful feet before my choice of polish was applied. And what a lovely sight they were, my (now) baby-soft tootsies, ready for their close-up.

What had I been waiting for?

I shall treat myself to pedicures forever. I shall forego soy lattes if I must in order to underwrite my monthly pedicure. Unlike a manicure, a pedicure will last a long time. Who knew that we are so much kinder to our toes than to our fingers? I didn't.

The treatment I received three weeks ago looks as good as it did when I left the salon. The only discernible difference? A teensy bit of new growth showing at the bottom. So for that reason alone, it'll soon be time for a redo even though the polish is still perfect.

If you've never had a pedicure, and have the negative attitude I did, consider opening yourself up to this refreshing experience. And there's an added bonus: Most pedicure chairs also provide massages.

17

To Heck with Tomorrow

I subscribe to an online Q & A site called Top Tips for Girls. It comes from England, and I first read about it in our daily paper. I assumed that Top Tips was geared to "girls" of all ages until the tips started arriving daily and I realized that they're primarily for young women with questions having to do with difficult mothers-in-law, straying boyfriends, and various cosmetic and weight-related dilemmas.

A recent questioner wanted to know what to do about a bunny boiler. A bunny boiler? In case you're one of the few remaining earthlings who haven't seen the film *Fatal Attraction* – and I'm one of them – a bunny boiler is a vengeful ex-wife or lover. Glenn Close's character boiled her ex-lover's daughter's pet rabbit out of spite. There aren't any bunny boilers in the crowd I hang out with. About all we boil is hot water for tea.

Regarding another Top Tip inquiry: "How to tell your parents you have lots of tattoos, and hence wedding dress shopping might not be as much fun as they expected," my question is: Did it never occur to that young lady that she might one day be wearing a wedding dress and that tattoos and a wedding dress might not be a good mix?

When I see people with tattoos covering their arms and legs and or even spread over their entire bodies, I realize that they're operating under a system of aesthetics that is utterly foreign to me – I will *never* understand it – and I wonder if they've ever considered how those tattoos will look when they're in their sixties.

In the semi-likely event that a tattoo wearer were to come to his or her senses and want their body to look normal again, I hope they realize that tattoos are removable only at great pain and expense via procedures such as dermabrasion – removing the top few layers of skin – or excision, cutting out the tattoo and sewing the surrounding skin together. Good grief.

A friend of ours who is retired from an executive position had his right arm tattooed while in the army. When he entered the business world he felt he could only wear long sleeves. It was a while before he mustered the confidence to shed his long sleeves and become involved in golf, the businessman's favorite networking vehicle.

It must be human nature to avoid looking ahead, to consider the consequences of our youthful decisions. The same lack of foresight that impels some people to decorate their bodies with gruesome images prevents others from looking ahead to their financial future. *Now* is the only thing that matters to them. Why worry about tomorrow?

This "I want it now; who cares about the consequences?" mindset has brought us to our current wobbly economic status. Too many of us want everything, *now,* to live like a rich person, *now*. It used to be we bought only things we could afford. But if you were to ask these people if they can *afford* a certain item, they'd look at you as if you were speaking a foreign language. To them, the language of thrift *is* a foreign language.

There was a time when most of us, if we were wise, had a savings account. We earned so much per week and put so much aside "for a rainy day." We gathered our spare change until we had enough to pay cash for that much-desired item. Apparently, most people today think that's a pretty lame way to go through life. They'd rather have $10,000 in credit card debt because they must have that 52-inch flat screen TV or Escalade or three-garage McMansion *now*.

And they *must* have that tattoo.

I'm glad I won't be around three or four decades from now to witness millions of old people, who didn't bother to think ahead, walking around with wrinkly, saggy, tattoos as they make their way to their post-retirement jobs to supplement their Social Security – if there still is such a thing.

18

How Much Can We Take?

For more seasons than I care to count, I've wondered why people still spend perfectly good time and money to witness the multi-season losing Pittsburgh Pirates engage in the sport of baseball. What motivates them to do so? The fancy new stadium? The unique view of the downtown skyscrapers? Free tickets?

It would probably be pretty effective if the public would put its collective foot down, stay home for a season and send a message to the owners that they will no longer tolerate the team's embarrassing performance. The public can survive without baseball, but baseball cannot survive without the public.

Unfortunately, the public, a good portion of it anyway, cannot survive without the airlines. The availability of rapid, long-distance travel has become woven into the fabric of our lives, and although some of us fly around the country and the world for fun, a good many of us really do need to get to distant places, and quickly.

At the beginning of each flying adventure, we must now empty our pockets, surrender our shoes, and practically disrobe in front of a roomful of strangers, a few of whom have the authority to do just about everything short of feeling us up. I stoically submit to this indignity when what I'd like to do is have the perpetrator cited for indecent assault.

Remember the good old days when we complained about the lousy meals we were served on airplanes? Wouldn't it be great to have one of those lousy meals now, built into the ticket price, instead of the carb-loaded junk they now purvey for six dollars or more, in boxes with cute names like Classic and Luxe, or the three dollar "a la carte" snacks – that description causes me to roll my eyes – such as tiny cans of ersatz potato chips, Oreo cookies, or mixed nuts? Remember those wonderful free peanuts?

These days, in order to have something to eat that resembles an actual meal, we are forced either to tote a sack of vittles from home – how classy is that? – or pay exorbitant prices at airport concession stands. We then have the choice of consuming these meals during our flight or devouring them in the waiting area with our fellow travelers who look so attractive stuffing their faces with pizza or sandwiches while trying to keep the ingredients from falling out and decorating the floor and their carry-on luggage.

The airlines, knowing that the passengers cannot go on strike, are sticking it to us any way they can. Among the recent outrages, charging passengers to check suitcases is among the more egregious. Imagine, going on a trip and wanting to take an actual suitcase of needed items. What temerity.

So what happens? Passengers bring refrigerator-sized carry-ons aboard the plane free of charge. This guarantees that a number of bags will have to be removed from the cabin and checked. The good news for those passengers? Their bags are checked free of charge. Sounds like a winner to me.

What next? Charging to use the onboard toilets? Don't laugh. The cheapie Irish carrier Ryanair is considering doing just that. CEO Michael O'Leary is touting the idea of putting a one-pound ($1.43) coin slot on the restroom doors as a means of raising "discretionary revenue." So it's only a matter of time. US Air and Delta know a good idea when they hear one. And if the government hasn't been able to stop the airlines from keeping us trapped on the tarmac for ten hours, don't expect them to protect us from being charged to use the facilities.

On a recent trip home from Oregon, my husband and I, for a mere seventy-seven dollars apiece, could have purchased an extra five inches of leg room on our flight to Chicago. That's around fifteen dollars an inch – a bargain to be sure. We passed. And when the passenger in front of me reclined his seat all the way back into my *New York Times* I thought, well at least we're saving a hundred fifty-four dollars.

And at the end of our long day of travel? We waited nearly an hour for our two suitcases for which we had paid forty dollars, each way, to check. The people with the oversized carry-ons were probably asleep in their beds by the time our bags came tumbling onto the carousel. Why the delay? We suspect there are too many baggage handlers on "furlough."

The airlines tell us that these measures are due to 9/11 and the struggling economy, and I believe that to a point. But the skeptic in me would never put it past the people running things, the ones who take home the big bucks for thinking up new ways to dehumanize us while they travel in the eight-thousand dollar business class seats, to squeeze us 'til we holler "Uncle" because they know they can get away with it.

Because we can't go on strike.

19

Obsolescence

In a recent issue of *New York* magazine about the aughts – the double-zero decade that we've just slogged through – there was a two-page pictorial, "Rust in Peace," which displayed items that have been a part of our lives for many years but were rendered obsolete during the last ten years. A few of them, such as the incandescent light bulb and the telephone book, are still hanging around. But their role and importance have shrunk and their days are numbered.

Others once hailed as cutting edge are fading away or gone altogether. Remember the floppy disk? The cassette tape? Is there anybody around besides my husband and me who still own cars that have cassette players?

Bank deposit slips are on the list of the moribund along with answering machines, foldable road maps, Hydrox cookies – really? – and *Playboy* magazine. *Playboy* magazine? What, no more centerfolds?

The fax machine beside me as I type this is becoming a victim of progress. Not long ago considered revolutionary, it is being replaced by scanners and Internet fax services that are cheaper, more secure, and more environmentally friendly. And they don't require special paper or take up valuable space in your office.

It used to be that when you bought something new you could look forward to enjoying it as state-of-the-art for a couple of decades. But during the last few years, advances in technology occurred at such a dizzying rate that it's unlikely you can buy an electronic device today that won't be headed for the heap of history in a year.

No matter how much we tell ourselves that we don't need these new gadgets and try to ignore them, when we finally get on board we wonder how we ever got along without them. That was certainly true of my first microwave. And I was skeptical about the TiVo. I wasn't even sure what it was. Then I read an article about a fellow who was at a complete loss when his TiVo went on the blink. So I bought one and immediately knew just how he felt. If you own a DVR (digital video recorder), which is what TiVo is, you, too, know exactly how he felt. If you don't own one, it would be kind of like suddenly having to do without your remote control.

A few generations ago, there were those who didn't want to be bothered with the newfangled telephone. What would they think of the 21st century smartphones, such as the iPhone, which can do just about everything but cook dinner? *The Post-Gazette*'s Adrian McCoy calls them the "Swiss Army knives of tech devices."

A cousin of mine pooh-poohed television back in the early fifties. Why would anybody want one of those? Then one day she went out and bought herself the fanciest Stromberg Carlson TV in the store. Back then, owning a Stromberg Carlson was like owning a Cadillac.

Eventually, most of us get on board and embrace the new technological wonders as they come down the pike. If that weren't the case we'd all still be driving cars with manual transmissions and listening to 78's on our Victrolas. Some of us remember what it was like to get up every five minutes to change the record.

When we finally do give in, we sign the sales receipt knowing that, like a new car, the device we've just bought will begin to depreciate the minute we walk out of the store.

It'll be interesting to see what gadgets the wheel of progress churns out in the next ten years and what kind of shelf life they'll have. By then, maybe they'll be disposable – like yesterday's newspaper.

20

Best Friends Forever?

Have you ever instantly hit it off with someone with whom you have such great rapport that you feel you could converse forever and never run out of things to talk about?

Many years ago, on tour with the orchestra, I left my favorite raincoat on the bus to the airport in Geneva and spent nearly all of our free day in Rome looking for a replacement.

Exhausted from my search I took a break in a café not far from the Victor Emmanuel monument and fell into conversation with a young Japanese woman named Fukuko. It turned out she was on vacation from her job with Scandinavian Airlines in Copenhagen. I don't remember what we talked about – our significant others, probably – but our conversation went on for so long that we ended up having dinner together in a Chinese restaurant. Imagine that – an African-American woman from Pittsburgh and a Japanese woman from Copenhagen hitting it off well enough to have dinner together at a Chinese restaurant, in Rome. Sounds like material for a sitcom.

We had a delightful time, and by the end of the evening I felt that I had a new BFF, a best friend forever, and maybe she felt the same way. We corresponded briefly after that, but the trans-Atlantic friendship faded. Email didn't exist back then to keep us within a "Send" or "Receive" of each other.

Every few years I try to find Fukuko online, but without success. Perhaps she acceded to what might have been her parents' wishes, to go back to Japan and find a prosperous man to marry.

A few years later, on vacation in Hawaii, I sat down at the Hilton guest services desk to a slightly brusque reception from the woman on duty. But something I said softened her up pretty fast and we ended up spending some pleasant hours together learning about each others' slightly unorthodox lives. She even found me a piano to practice on in the hotel ballroom.

Julie was from New York, probably Jewish, and married to a Hawaiian. I chatted with her on the phone once after we got home, but from such a distance that friendship also fell by the wayside. But recently, with the help of WhitePages.com, I tracked her down after typing in a host of different spellings of her unusual Hawaiian last name. I wrote her a letter but never heard back from her.

I suspect that these BFF friendships are a "girl thing." Men don't seem to relate by happenstance the way women do. Perhaps females are historically connected because they've been in the same boat ever since Eve wondered what an apple tasted like and got us all into trouble.

It's probably just as well that these friendships have an expiration date. What they say might be true: familiarity breeds contempt. If not contempt, then perhaps just disappointment. If we were to find out much more about our BFFs, we might discover that they're not as perfect as they seemed at first.

These fleeting friendships, however temporary, are refreshing. They sail into our lives like a cool breeze, and then, like dust, are gone with the wind. What remains are lovely lifetime memories.

And who knows? A new BFF might be the next person who walks through the door.

21

The following, although a departure in mood from the essays that surround it, is a tribute to one of my favorite characteristics of human speech.

The Noble Schwa

We all use it but few of us know what it's called. It's the *e* in mother, the *ou* in generous. Webster defines it as "a weak, neutral vowel sound occurring in most of the unstressed syllables in English speech, as the *a* in alone, the *e* in happen or the *u* in circus." It's nearly impossible to utter a sentence without using it, yet this little character that looks like an upside-down e doesn't appear on the keyboards of most typewriters or computers, and it's the rare individual who knows what it is. Most people see it every time they open a dictionary, but they don't know what it's called.

This little character – ə – is the phonetic symbol called *schwa*. Its name comes from the Hebrew *shewa*, described as the "obscure vowel, sometimes represented by : and transliterated as an italicized *e*." Without neighboring consonants, its sound is that of a mere grunt. To write down its pronunciation, *shwaah*, is easier than doing so for most of the words in which it is heard, because it doesn't contain any schwas.

My affection for this mighty mite began at Carnegie Mellon University where all freshman music majors were required to study phonetics with Oleta Ben, queen mother of the music school. Most of my fellow students thought it was a dumb course – as useless, in their opinions, as Latin or a sixth toe. But I loved it and found being able to write symbols to indicate exactly how a word should be pronounced fascinating and even liberating. I spent many an idle hour turning prose, poetry, even names and addresses into phonetic symbols. I suspect that even Mrs. Ben considered my enthusiasm for phonetics a bit odd. And I was immersed in all of this before the expression "Get a life!" had been thought up.

I soon discovered that a friend from music camp days – a proper young lady from Baltimore with the proper-sounding name of Helen Twiss – loved phonetics as much as I did. So she and I launched a correspondence, using phonetics exclusively, which lasted until we wore ourselves out.

Of all the symbols in the Standard American English phonetic alphabet, the *schwa* is my undisputed favorite. That's quite an accomplishment in a family of such interesting and useful symbols. It's too bad that we Americans are unwilling or unable to acknowledge the function of the schwa. For instance, that is demonstrated by the way we say Meineke. The original owners of that name did not have a "key" at the end. There should be two *schwa* sounds in Meineke – MINE-uh-kuh (sort of). And the first name of actress Demi Moore should be pronounced "duh-MEE –the French word for half, not DEM-i (as in demigod). The *e* in her name is a *schwa*. Her name is Demetria (də-MEE-tree-ə).

Have you ever tried to write, using ordinary printed letters, the pronunciation of a word? How would you represent circus? SIR-kis? I would read that SIR-kiss. SIR-kus? Looks like that profane nobleman, Sir Cuss. How to pronounce the word happen? HAP-pin? HAP-pen? Would either of those do the job? Not really. With the means at our disposal, we can make only imprecise attempts at representing the accurate pronunciation of words because the vowel sounds, resonant by definition, last too long.

If I still haven't convinced you of the usefulness of this odd little symbol, try writing down the pronunciation of *melodramatic* without using the schwa. Good luck. Here's what it looks like using the *schwa*: me-lə-drə-MA-t ək. Neat and unambiguous.

Maybe I'll launch a crusade on behalf of the hard-working but unappreciated schwa, design a petition, make signs and organize a march on the makers of electronic keyboards. "GIVE US A SCHWA!" and "SCHWA POWER!" Or "HURRAH FOR THE SCHWA!"

Dear me. I didn't mean to get so carried away. Well, if nothing else, I hope my impassioned testimony on behalf of the schwa has given you something to think about – a *schwa*-sized nugget of information – rather than rolling your eyes and making circles around your temple with your index finger.

Gee. Just as talking about food makes me hungry, all of this has given me the urge to cook up a few paragraphs of phonetics, liberally peppered with schwas.

Now, if I can just find a current address for Helen Twiss...

22

How Does It Work?

My husband gave me a smart phone for Christmas. It's an amazing device. By means of a touch screen, I can check and answer my email, read a variety of publications, listen to hundreds of radio stations, store my grocery list, take photos *or* videos and send them to people, Google all over the place, and get turn by turn GPS directions. And, oh yes – I can also make phone calls.

And although I know how to perform a fair number of functions on it, as is the case with my computer, there are even more I haven't figured out. It is so bursting with *apps* – applications – useful sites that one can access practically by blowing on the screen, that I'd challenge anyone, including the developer, to know what all of them do. Some of these devices contain 100,000 or more apps.

A few weeks ago I started writing a list of questions to ask the next time I was near a branch of a store that sells my phone. So when a new one displayed its "OPEN" sign in a brand new shopping center, I stopped in, at 10 a.m., knowing I'd have a specialist to myself.

Naturally, the list was still at home on my kitchen counter. But I remembered enough of the questions to

110

use up a half hour of the employee's time. He works there and should be an expert, right? Well yes, and he knows plenty. But, when I asked him if there was something I could touch to delete the 293 items in my email trash bin all at once he couldn't figure out how to do it. Is it possible that the brilliant designers of this device *forgot* to include a Delete Trash function among all those apps? I wonder how many can accumulate in there. A thousand? A billion? An infinite number?

Just before winter, we got a new furnace. It's a nice furnace, keeps the house warmer than the old furnace, and might have trimmed our gas bill by a few dollars. But neither my husband nor I have made much progress in operating the thermostat. We're from the ON/OFF school of electrical devices; anything more complicated makes us anxious. The thermostat has a timer, which, in the hands of someone who can understand written directions, will turn the furnace down when we go to bed, and turn it back on a few hours before we get up in the morning. But we haven't figured out how to make it do that. There are even directions inside the lid but we just don't *get* them. So we manually turn it down to 66 at night and back up to 72 in the morning. We're wasting all of that fancy digital capability by using our own digits.

We grew up in the age when appliances had ON/OFF switches, knobs that turn clockwise and counter-clockwise, or maybe a bar that slid to the right or left. There were no buttons to push until something flashed, and then push it again and something else flashed, and then push it again and it unflashed what was flashing. So back to the beginning.

I am not a Luddite, one of those people who refuses to get involved with anything new. Far from it. I *love* new things. As I sit here shortly after the rollout of the iPad, I'm wondering how long my fingers and wallet will itch before I run out to buy one.

I'm joined at the hip to my computer and consider myself a genuinely skilled intermediate user. But I spend far too much time puzzling over procedures that a twelve-year-old kid could figure out in ten seconds.

It's apparent that one reaches plateaus on this learning curve of technology. Just when we think we're up to speed, along comes a new, whizzier toy to ramp up our tech stress level, while our brains haven't had enough time to process what's already in there.

But we'd better all get on board this bandwagon that is dragging some of us, kicking and screaming, into this new age. The day is coming when all transactions and communication will take place in cyberspace, and if you skip the tutorial, you'll feel like the person with two left feet who's up next on *Dancing with the Stars*.

23

Why Doesn't She Write About Music?

Nobody has asked me that question, but a few have probably wondered. Perhaps they've thought it would be impolite to ask, that it would be intrusive. I don't know if that's true, but I certainly wouldn't want to be made to feel guilty or remiss because of what I *don't* write.

Non-musical topics occur to me with more frequency than musical topics. I'm struck by a subject, usually while still in bed. I leap up, rush into my office, and the words tumble onto my computer screen as a pretty much finished creation. Handel is said to have composed the "Messiah" in his head, during a stay at a friend's summer cottage, before he ever took pen to paper. That must be true. He finished it in twenty-four days. Just writing down all of those notes wouldn't have given him much time to stop and figure things out. He was depressed at the time, as was Rachmaninoff just before he wrote the magnificent Second Piano Concerto, which is his most beloved composition and whose theme is the basis of the song "Full Moon and Empty Arms." Depression can have its positive outcomes.

There, I've written something about music.

Obviously I'm fond of music. I've been playing it, on a variety of instruments, for more than sixty years.

I've listened to all kinds of music – much of which I've liked, some of which I haven't – for my entire life. But I don't feel compelled to write about it to the exclusion of everything else. And I believe that the oh-so-worldly, sophisticated people who read what I write are just as interested in non-musical topics as I am.

Actually, I *have* written about music, a lot. For seven years in the late '80s and early '90s, I edited and published a nationally distributed newsletter whose purpose was to raise awareness of talented African-American symphony musicians. I was also a contributor to *Symphony*, the publication of ICSOM, the International Conference of Symphony and Opera Musicians. But on a day to day basis my interests are eclectic. The humorous, the serious, and everything in between make it onto my list of possible topics.

I'm fascinated by those situations that most of us experience, regardless of our profession or expertise. What motivates people to do the things they do? How are we adjusting to the changes in our lives? How has technology affected us? What does it feel like to get older?

I'm a news junkie but I don't write much about current events because I'd probably get myself into trouble. Plus, there are already too many people weighing in on topics of the day – many of which they don't understand, but that doesn't stop them – via hundreds of blogs. My topics will continue to shoot in from left field, right field, and who knows, maybe even the field of music.

Speaking of which, every once in a while someone asks me to name my favorite composer. I realize they're trying to relate to the world of classical music, to show an interest. But when I'm not feeling especially generous, I might say to them, "Gee, I don't know. What is your favorite country?" (I've been asked that, too.) How can one possibly answer that question? It's like asking, "What is your favorite food?"

There are so many composers whose music I love that it would be impossible to pick *one*. If I answered Mozart, what then would happen to Rachmaninoff and Dvorak, Bach, Beethoven and Brahms, Schumann and Mahler, Debussy and Ravel – and some of the moderns? What is more sublime than the slow movement of the now-classic violin concerto by Samuel Barber?

If I were stranded on a desert island what music would I want to listen to day after day? Probably Bach and Mozart. Maybe a little Mendelssohn. Their music possesses clarity, like the blue ocean that would surround me. Living on a diet of the romantic Russians or Germans might be bearable for a while, but eventually I'd be towed under by such heavy fare.

24

Cars

My first car, a gift from my parents when I graduated from college, was a 1963 metallic blue Dodge Dart, certainly not a car I would have chosen if it had been up to me. It didn't suit my image of myself – although it probably seemed like just the right car to those who saw the real me and not my fantasy self. My father, who was sixty-eight at the time, was friends with a gentleman who sold cars as a sideline. He must have made my father an offer on that Dart that he couldn't refuse.

Not to say that I wasn't thrilled to have a car of my own. No more buses. No more depending on other people. Autonomy, in its most literal sense, was mine.

That was barely a year before the Mustang came out. Now *that* was a car. I could picture myself cruising around in a white Mustang convertible, scarf trailing in the wind like Snoopy. The '64 Mustang has secured its place in history as one of the grooviest cars of all time, and at the age of twenty-two I would have loved to feel a little groovier than I did in a Dodge Dart.

My next car was more like it – a 1968 Mercury Cougar XR-7 in diamond blue with a black vinyl roof – a real stunner, built on the Mustang platform.

One sunny afternoon, after a Pittsburgh Symphony young people's concert, I went to the parking lot at the Masonic Temple in Oakland and couldn't find my beautiful Cougar. It was a huge parking lot, so it was half an hour before I had to admit that my beautiful Cougar had vanished. Someone, probably a kid from the nearby high school, had driven it right out of the lot. It was found the next day, in a not-so-nice neighborhood, missing its radio and a complete season of Pittsburgh Symphony tickets. I hope the perp enjoyed the concerts.

Next car, the most gorgeous: a 1974 Olds Cutlass Supreme in Viking blue with a white vinyl roof for which I special-ordered a 455 engine. Don't tell me I didn't look cool driving that car.

But one night, while I was visiting a friend who lived on a busy city street, we heard a crash as somebody plowed into my Viking blue beauty. Not long after that I sold it, reluctantly. Someone wiser than I suggested that the frame might be broken.

There are still a few of those Cutlasses around, and they still look amazingly up-to-date.

I'm fascinated by the role cars play in our lives. They say so much about us – who we are or who we'd like to be. In the *Bloomberg News* Doron Levin wrote: "Cars are the way many American drivers express themselves, as reflective of their owners' personalities as the clothes they wear." How true.

We have two cars, a ten-year-old luxury sedan with barely fifty thousand miles, and an eight-year-old middle-of-the-road SUV with normal mileage. Out of sheer

117

boredom, I would love to have a new vehicle, but I can't figure out what I want. Used to be I'd see a car and think, I *must* have one of those. But that doesn't happen anymore, either because of creeping ennui or because there is such a dizzying array of choices.

I'd like a vehicle that represents me in just the right way. If it's too fancy it might turn off my friends, plus it will make my wardrobe and house look tired. I love my SUV and would like another. But each one I've tried has a down side, like the one whose upholstery is such a light color, even in the cargo area – where I stash garbage cans and other grimy things – that I can picture its being ready for the Rug Doctor within a week.

So round and round I go, from dealer to dealer, from web page to web page, waiting for my next vehicle to call my name. However, if the stock market keeps bouncing around at its current rate, I might decide to sell both cars and get myself a used Daewoo. There's a nice 1999 Daewoo Lano online for $600 or, if I'm feeling flush, maybe I'll be the first in our neighborhood to buy a brand new Tata Nano, the world's cheapest car, from India, for $2500.

25

Still Listening

I don't remember precisely what the gentleman had suggested to incur my wrath, but when I was a member of the Lemington Elementary School orchestra, I kicked the music teacher, Mr. Horelick, in the shin. That kick must have gotten it out of my system because, in my ensuing forty-plus year career as an orchestra musician, I managed never to kick another conductor in the shin, or anywhere else, although the temptation must have at times been nearly irresistible.

I'm telling you this because the result of my toe to Mr. Horelick's shin was the worst possible punishment: My mother removed my radio from my room for six weeks. I would much rather have been tarred and feathered or pilloried in the town square.

Unlike other little girls who were attached to their dolls, I was attached to my radio as I listened to *The Great Gildersleeve, Fibber McGee and Molly,* and even shoot 'em ups like *The Big Story,* with its "Ein Heldenleben" ("A Hero's Life") theme music. Not until years later did I learn that "Ein Heldenleben" is a bona fide concert hall favorite by Richard Strauss, composer of the *2001: A Space Odyssey* music.

Another of my favorites was Pittsburgh's and the country's very first telephone call-in talk show, *Party Line* with Ed and Wendy King. Back then, before the development of the seven-second delay, the listeners could hear only Ed and Wendy's side of the conversation as they summarized the callers' questions. Even in the relatively benign 50s it was too risky to turn just anybody loose on the public airwaves. That seems quaint to us now, when angry hosts and outraged callers have at each other with practically no holds barred. Profanity is still frowned upon, but anything else goes.

I still listen to radio talk for several hours a day, but in increasingly non-traditional ways. For instance, for those in the Pittsburgh area who were fans of Lynn Cullen or Doug Hoerth on a succession of radio stations over the years, there's good news and bad news. The good news is that Lynn can still be heard, and also *seen*, Monday through Friday on the Pittsburgh City Paper's web site. And although *Lynn Cullen Live* is broadcast from 10 to 11 a.m., you can listen to it on your computer via podcasts, *any time* of the day or night.

The bad news is that Doug Hoerth seems to have fallen into the black hole of obscurity. That's a shame because, love him or hate him, Doug was interesting, funny, and staggeringly knowledgeable about a variety of topics. And there was no better interviewer.

A nationally syndicated talk show that, unfortunately, is not available on a local station – I urge you to go to the web site and sample it online – is Doug Stephan's *Good Day*. In this age of angry partisanship, *Good Day* is the proverbial breath of fresh air. Stephan, who broadcasts from his farm in Maine, holds forth five mornings a week along with a studio full of amusing co-hosts and interesting guests. The topics run the gamut from silly to serious. Doug Stephan is a genial host with a long and unusual history in the medium.

I listen to *Good Day* on my "Droid" (my Motorola Android smartphone), using an app called Stitcher, which is free to download and will lead you to *hundreds* of interesting podcasts such as "Books on the Nightstand," a useful Internet presence during which the hosts describe books they've read and enjoyed that you will probably never have time to read.

I recently learned some interesting facts, via "Books on the Nightstand," about Harper Lee who wrote *To Kill a Mockingbird*. This year marks the fiftieth anniversary of the book. At eighty-four, Harper Lee is still living in the town where she and Truman Capote were born and became fast friends, Monroeville, Alabama. And although she emerges to accept an important award now and then, she hasn't granted an interview since 1964.

At the risk of bogging you down with too many suggestions, I'd be remiss if I didn't tell you about two other excellent programs that you can listen to in real time or online at your leisure. *The Commonwealth Club of California* describes itself as "the nation's oldest and largest public affairs forum," and features a variety of speakers, always brilliant guests who are making a difference in the world. The show is broadcast on various NPR stations including Pittsburgh's WDUQ-FM, now

WESA-FM, on Sundays from 6 to 7 a.m. Check your local listings.

Another excellent one is *On the Media* with Brooke Gladstone and Bob Garfield. The show takes an objective look at how the news is covered by the print and electronic media.

Maybe none of this interests you in the least. Maybe you'd rather go to the dentist than listen to radio talk. But this (until recently) low-tech medium provides some of the most rewarding hours of my day, and, after nearly six decades, I'm still listening. And I suspect that, when I'm ready to cash in my chips, the last thing they'll pry from my "cold, dead hands" – in the words of Charlton Heston – will be my radio.

Since writing this I have discovered the wide variety of programming available via podcasts, which I listen to on my iPad. No more AM talk radio for me.

Doug Hoerth passed away in 2011. His radio show, which was his life, had been canceled, and I will always believe that he died of a broken heart.

26

Close Calls

One evening, not long ago, our lives came within inches of changing in a big way. My husband and I were heading to a restaurant, near Pittsburgh's Carnegie Music Hall, to grab a quick dinner before attending a lecture. I was driving. Facing two lanes of oncoming traffic at a familiar intersection, I prepared to make a left turn. A bus had stopped in the center lane and I was focused on the curb lane in case the bus obscured oncoming vehicles.

I whipped around to the left and there, a few feet from my headlights, was a woman, eyes wide with terror, caught in the intersection. I'll never forget the freeze-frame look on her face. She resumed her pace on wobbly legs but looked back at me with the terror of someone who has come close to being crushed like a bug under tons of steel, driven by me.

I drove on. Close call.

Except for a few inches, many lives would have been turned inside out that evening. And as I thought through the incident in the minutes following, I wondered what the appropriate reaction should be. Should I have thanked God? My guardian angel? *Her* guardian angel? I felt that I should react in some way beyond continuing life as usual. It didn't seem right to dismiss a near catastrophe without a proper amount of self-recrimination and gratitude.

As I maneuvered through the traffic, I kept imagining the scene at that intersection if the worst had happened – red and blue police car lights spinning wildly as rush hour gawkers slowed down to observe something gory to report at the dinner table; an ambulance shrieking to the site; the interrogation of driver, passenger and witnesses. I visualized the notification of the victim's family, their heartbreak and their rage at me.

Could my life ever be the same? Should it?

We cannot know, during the course of each day, how close we come to meeting our Maker. I'll never forget the night that a woman who had been attending a symphony concert at Pittsburgh's Heinz Hall was crushed against the side of the building by a car that had shot out of the parking lot across the street. Reports said that the gas pedal had become stuck. People that I knew, wives of orchestra members, were walking along that sidewalk, towards the stage door, before the tragedy occurred. How their minds must have reeled for the next few days until the realization of how close they had come to the end faded into memory.

We pass our days confident that bad things happen to *other* people, preferring not to acknowledge our own vulnerability. We don't get out of bed each morning thinking, "This might be *the* day," although I must confess that I stick to the curb lane on a few local roads that have seen their share of head-on collisions. Why tempt fate?

Our ability to rationalize shields us from thinking the unthinkable. I suspect that the young men and women who voluntarily go off to war nurture a romantic notion of what it will be like, reassuring themselves that others, not they, will fall under the bullet or the bomb. And none of us is prepared, or ever will be, to fall victim to a terrorist attack. Terrorists kill *other* people.

When I sit down for my morning meditation, I give thanks for the previous day's safe passage through the many miles I've driven and the many unseen hazards I've escaped. I have deluded myself into thinking that my gratitude will protect me.

Today is a new day. Nothing bad is going to happen. And when I finish writing this, I will sally forth, into the morning sun, confident that although a close call is always possible, my day will not end in tragedy. Nor will yours.

27

Coupon Clipping

Why do I *do* it?

There's a ritual that takes place in our house every Sunday morning. I fetch the newspaper from beneath the prickly pyracantha bush, at the risk of shredding my bathrobe, hustle the paper into the basement and dump all the superfluous stuff directly into the trash. Up goes the rest to the breakfast table as I grab a pair of scissors and ready myself to examine – not the opinion pages, not reports of world events or business news, not even the week's cultural events. My target? The coupon booklets. There's MONEY in them thar pages!

What is it about clipping coupons that is so alluring to me when I think nothing – well not quite nothing – of spending eight or nine dollars on a half-filled glass of wine in a trendy new bistro? I must be nuts, right? Maybe so, but a dollar off a couple of tubes of my favorite toothpaste is a mini-bonanza, a dollar saved to spend on something else. And it's a sure thing, unlike the Powerball lottery where millions of optimists deposit their dollars into a bottomless pit with no hope of winning mega-millions. I think you'd agree that a one in 350 million chance is no hope of winning.

We all want something for nothing – or at least for less. That's why the super stores, despite their reputation for despoiling the landscape and knocking the stuffings out of small-town America, have been so wildly success-ful. The promise of getting more for less is irresistible. When I leave one of those places, I enjoy a momentary sense of triumph, that little thrill of putting something over on the system. Even the drivers of the Cadillacs and BMWs in the parking lot are not immune from the wish to save a dollar here, a dollar there.

A few years ago I read *The Prize Winner of Defiance, Ohio: How My Mother Raised 10 Kids on 25 Words or Less,* by Terry Ryan. It was about a woman who was strug-gling with ten children and an alcoholic husband. If she hadn't won prizes, large and small, by submitting box tops, soaked-off labels, and winning lines for jingles, her family would have literally starved to death. (The book was made into a film with Julianne Moore and Woody Harrelson.)

Jingle-writing contests have gone the way of rabbit ears, which leaves coupon clipping as one of the few remaining relics of our post-Depression, penny-pinch-ing past. And heaven knows, even in 2010, being able to shave two or three dollars off the price of a bag of groceries has its appeal, whether the shopper is on a budget or not.

But even I have my limits. I seldom clip a coupon that's worth less than 40 cents, nor will I clip anything that requires me to buy more than two of whatever it is. And, unless they're for a substantial amount, I don't go in for rebates. By the time you assemble the proof-of-purchase documentation and pay postage to mail in the rebate coupon, you've used up more time than the rebate is worth. If they *really* want my business, maybe they should just knock off a few bucks.

There are a few die-hards who don't bother with coupons. One friend, who is in her sixties, claims never to have clipped a coupon in her life. She is too afraid of becoming "as annoying as those folks with envelopes full of coupons, half of them expired, who require triple time in the check-out line."

But there are plenty of conscientious coupon-clippers who have profited big time, including a lady who figures that she saved twenty-five dollars a week during the eighteen years that her twin sons were growing up. That totaled a whopping $23,000, plus interest. That's a lotta corn flakes!

I suspect that the real reason I clip coupons – besides the fact that it's fun to see how neatly I can cut along the dotted lines – is that it deludes me into believing, despite all evidence to the contrary, that I am a thrifty person. I watch my pennies keeping in mind that, as the old folks used to say, "Pennies make dollars."

In this era, when an embarrassing percentage of Americans are up to their eyeballs in debt, a little old-fashioned penny-pinching is becoming a necessity. Where to start? The coupon pages are as good a place as any.

28

Life in a Small Space

My husband and I recently took a journey of more than 4,000 miles across Canada, most of it by train. When we signed up for this adventure – the Trans Canada Rail Odyssey and the Rockies – we didn't have a clear picture of what we were in for. It sounded like a fabulous trip, and in many ways it was. But we didn't realize, because the brochure scrupulously avoided telling us, that for the longest leg of the trip we would be existing in a train compartment that measured seven by seven feet. We were told to bring only our carry-on bags packed with sufficient clothing and necessities for three days and nights, and when we opened the door we could see why: It would have been the suitcases or us, not both.

Our compartment consisted of two bunk beds, a tiny toilet room with barely enough space for our knees, and a small sink with faucets like the ones on airplanes that stop the minute you let go. There was no flat surface on which to place anything, so everything we used had to be put immediately back into its place in our luggage.

During the day, the beds could be stored in the walls to unearth two armchairs. But we knew from the beginning that we wouldn't be spending any more time than necessary in that claustrophobic cubicle, when there were seating areas nearby with more space and light, and also a couple of cars with tables for games and visiting with other passengers. So we left our beds in place in case we wanted to crawl in for a nap in the afternoon.

As a double, our accommodations were luxurious compared with the accommodations for single travelers whose compartments had one pull-down bed which, when opened, denied the occupant access to the toilet. Can you imagine? If that unfortunate individual needed to answer the call of nature in the middle of the night, he or she either had to hike up the bed or stumble down the corridor to a communal restroom.

Our compartment was supplied with two plastic drawstring sacks, each containing two bath towels, a washcloth, soap and shampoo. The shower, located at the end of the corridor, was activated by a push button and was amazingly efficient. And it didn't hurt that our compartment was the closest to the shower.

I was the one who got to climb the narrow ladder into the stratosphere, and I always made sure that I had everything I needed for the night before launching my assault on the summit.

On the first night we heard some little noises coming from the next compartment. Then I heard a sneeze. I said "Gezundheit," in a not very loud voice. A little voice came back, "Thank you." So we knew that, despite the rumble of the train, the walls were thin and that if we didn't wish to be overheard we'd better converse *sotto voce.*

This experience taught us a lesson about how adaptable we human beings are. What seemed impossible on Day One actually began to be sort of fun by Day Two. It tested not only our ingenuity but also the degree to which we could coexist peaceably in cramped quarters. My husband joked that it reminded him of the isolation chambers in which they test astronauts to determine their compatibility over prolonged periods in outer space.

In this bigger is better world, we managed to exist quite nicely in a minimum of space with a minimum of necessities. And I have to say that once I climbed the ladder, I rather enjoyed snuggling under the duvet in my little above-ground nook and being jostled to sleep by the motion of the train as it sped across the Canadian prairies.

And ooooh, that whistle blowin' in the night...

29

Letter to Dr. Laura

Dr. Laura:

I've written to you only once although I listen to you often, not because I agree with everything you say – I don't – but because I'm amazed by your ability to cut to the heart of an issue and keep callers on track. I also listen because it's always interesting to hear other people's problems. Their difficulties make our own seem insignificant.

Although I realize that it's part of your "method," it is nevertheless fascinating to me that the contemptuous tone with which you address some callers doesn't prompt them to tell you to go f–k yourself, or to say, "How *dare* you speak to me that way!"

That said, my reaction to your recent "gaffe" was to scratch my head and think, "Now she's gone too far." And it wasn't long after that that you disappeared from the airwaves.

Comparing you to Tiger Woods is something I would never have imagined myself doing. But you and he seem to be similarly clueless. He thought he could beat the cyber-system – that ever-present possibility of instantaneous transmission of anything we do or say by way of electronic devices. And you believed, perhaps

132

because of what you consider your position of entitlement, that you could say *anything* on the air, that you had a free pass.

Until I heard the call I'm writing about, I thought that perhaps people were over-reacting. Then I listened to it. It was bad. Continuous repetition of the N-word was bad enough. But then you forged ahead, adding insult to injury with your advice.

I am an African-American woman, happily married to a white man for twenty-six years. I have never experienced a moment of anything but respect and affection from his family or his friends. But if I had, and had asked a professional (or anyone else) for advice about mistreatment or insults, I would have been dumbfounded to be told that I'm too sensitive and that if I couldn't take the heat, I shouldn't have gone into the kitchen. If everyone refused to confront uncomfortable or difficult situations we would all still be living in caves – in some foreign land.

Although I am a classical pianist, I have occasion to improvise popular songs, and once in a while I play a wrong note or chord when I shouldn't *go* there. You improvise on the air, and, as you thrashed about for advice for that caller, you should not have *gone* there.

I hope that, in the midst of licking your wounds, you have learned a lesson. There are some words that even you, Dr. Laura, simply cannot utter with impunity on the public airwaves. If the caller had told you that her in-laws call her the C-word, would you have responded, "Well, anybody who has seen *The Vagina Monologues* has heard a whole auditorium of people shouting the C-word – 'C-word, C-word, C-word'! Do you think maybe you're being too sensitive?"

Somehow I don't think you would have.

30

Clean vs. Clutter

If it weren't for occasional company, I'd never clean house. That might be exaggeration, but if the prospect of the doorbell ringing doesn't motivate my husband and me to whip our abode into shape, I don't know what does. We get used to our own dust and clutter. But there's a strange phenomenon – is it the Law of Inverse Proportion? –which dictates that the closer the time comes for the doorbell to ring, the more visible become the fingerprints, cobwebs, and dust. And don't even mention the windows.

And although the company will never see it, I worry that I might be some lesser breed of human because of the jumble inside my drawers, the chaos of my closets, and the boxes and bags of *stuff* in the basement that I'd rather not have seen even by the mice that forage there for sustenance. Much of the assortment consists of boxes and bags of items from my late mother's house that would have been a shame to discard.

I suspect that a good many basements are like ours – filled with the combined detritus of multiple households through marriage, death, or kids with expensive educations moving back home. No wonder there's been an explosion of storage facilities. Instead of getting rid of our stuff, we just find it an apartment of its own that we get to pay for, year in and year out. This makes room for more *stuff* in our houses. Despite the abundance of trash we drag out for weekly pickup, or the occasional trip to Goodwill, we still hang on to too much – clothes we will never wear, dishes we will never use, books we will never finish. It obviously provides us with a degree of comfort and security, like a whale ensconced in an extra layer of blubber.

I'm a stasher of the "any port in a storm" variety, depositing items anywhere they'll fit, whether it makes sense or not. This results in some pretty weird assortments. In one kitchen drawer there are batteries, book matches, the directions for the veggie steamer, a moisture meter for plants, three tape measures, denture tablets for dissolving the crud in cut-flower vases, the shredding disc for my food processor, and two sets of foam rubber ear plugs. Although it sounds like the drawer of a crazy person, I suspect that many of you reading this have a couple of drawers just like it – the drawer version of sweeping dust under the rug.

No matter how much chaos lurks behind my closet doors and drawer fronts, it comforts me to know that I'm nothing like the people featured on TLC's *Hoarding: Buried Alive,* whose accumulating of *stuff* has gone from being garden variety eccentricity to full-blown pathology. Hoarding is a diagnosed mental disorder that is extremely difficult to treat. Some of the subjects are compulsive shoppers who buy clothes and jewelry far in excess of what they could ever use. Others are compulsive keepers who are gripped by unbearable anxiety at the notion of discarding anything – even a used Band-Aid.

We have a friend whose kitchen isn't much bigger than a bathroom. You would think he'd do his best to keep as much clutter as possible out of this minuscule space in order to give himself a few more inches of working surface. But instead, he keeps every plastic bag, every plastic container, and every foil pan that has ever crossed his threshold stacked in every available corner. He has plastic bags *stuffed* with plastic bags. When asked about it, he offers the excuse that he's saving the plastic containers for art classes at the school up the street. Yeah, right. In my opinion his clutter is a classic case of compulsive hoarding.

The closest I've come to hoarding is my collection of shopping bags. I keep all but the most pedestrian ones and have them arranged by size, season, and purpose. You'll have to agree that shopping bags have come a long way since the days of the utilitarian brown bag whose sole purpose was to carry home the groceries. One day a clever marketing person had the bright idea to put store names and logos on shopping bags to advertise their merchants' businesses. As bags became more elaborate, they became status symbols and collectors' items. In 1978, the Cooper-Hewitt Museum in New York City mounted an exhibit of one-hundred twenty-five shopping bags, which has since grown to a thousand.

We all have our eccentricities, some of which, unfortunately, are visible only to the people driven crazy by them. Whatever mine may be, compulsive housecleaning is not one of them.

The last time we entertained, to spare my back the usual amount of bending and lifting, I didn't do as much cleaning. And you know what? The world didn't stop spinning. If a guest happened to spot a cobweb in a corner or a smudge on the oven door, it's doubtful they decided not to come to our house again.

So we'll live with the clutter, run the sweeper before the doorbell rings, serve the company the best dinner and conversation we can muster – but keep them out of the basement.

31

Poetry

I have a problem with poetry. At least I have a problem with poetry that is all imagery but lacks rhyme and meter. If that makes me an illiterate twit, so be it. Most of the poems in the Saturday morning paper leave me scratching my head. "What does it *mean*?" I ask my husband, who doesn't get it, either. The imagery put forth is obviously intended for intellects more evolved than ours.

It seems that until relatively recently in the history of literary composition, rhyming was an accepted poetic device:

> *I burn my candle at both ends*
> *It will not last the night.*
> *But, ah my foes, and oh, my friends*
> *It gives a lovely light.*
>   (Edna St. Vincent Millay)

Even Shakespeare wrote in rhyme and meter:

> *Gaze where you should, and that will clear your sight.*
> *As good to wink, sweet love, as look on night.*
>   *(A Comedy of Errors)*

But to the cognoscenti anything that rhymes is considered *verse* not *poetry*. In the early 1950s, my mother, Helen Prattis, wrote nearly three-hundred poems under the heading "Everyday Verse," for the *Pittsburgh Courier* when my editor father suggested she do so.

In the late '80s I sent samples of her work to Samuel Hazo, Pittsburgh's reigning poetry maven. His reaction was less than effusive; he described my mother's writings, somewhat dismissively, as *verse*, not *poetry*. Well, excuuuse me.

All of my mother's verses rhymed and used meter – except one, "A Warning," her sole foray into blank, or "free" verse. Here's the first verse, which she described as:

(A journey into free verse – or worse.)

According to the laws
Of "natural selection"
And that awesome business
Of "recapitulation of the species,"
As cathode-ray tubes mesmerize
And dazzle
And televiewers watch the screen
And listen,

People probably some day will be
All eyes and ears!

And one of her rhyming verses titled "Hilly Home Town":

The tourist can't suppress a grin
At what seems quite insane to him,
To see a level street until,
Quite suddenly, it climbs a hill.

A perpendicular one, too,
That boasts a panoramic view
And makes the city, full of lights
A fairy land when viewed at night.

That tourist's spent a lot of time
In other places, other climes
He's seen some awe-inspiring sights
But none like our town, seen at night.

A friend sent a recently published book of his poems that I really wanted to love and understand. I did *get* a few, but most of them left me baffled. A little additional explanation from him, via email, cleared away some of my puzzlement.

Which brings me to my own journey into free verse, which, frankly, is the reason I've written the last several paragraphs. I wrote the following in 1996 and drag it out every October, come hell or high water. I have no idea if it's any good. It probably isn't vague enough to satisfy the standards of real poets. But I like it, and, in the end, isn't that all that matters?

Credit for the title goes to my husband Charlie who inspires me with his flashes of brilliance:

Season in a Minor Key

It is a morning like no other.
A change is in the air.
The sun no longer cheers me;
It casts an eerie, melancholy light.
This morning I can no longer deny
That beloved summer is dying.

Fall is riding in on blustery breezes
That thumb their windy noses at my
Summer-thinned blood and chill me to the core.

I reach into my closet for a wrap
To insulate myself
Against the unwelcome guest
And switch the thermostat from
"Cool" to "Heat."
And think about how long it will be there.

An all-day-soaker rain, and another,
and another
Seem to wash away the light,
Sending it into the rising rivers,
Taking with it what remains
Of the warmth and the beauty of summer.

Low-hanging slate-gray clouds
Create an ominous primeval light upon the landscape.
It looks like the end of the world.

142

In One Era And Out The Other

Summer plays a sprightly scherzo of a tune;
But fall, a latter movement of the seasonal sonata,
Is scored as an adagio,
In a mournful, minor key.

But wait.
Golden sunlight
Warms my blood today.
Is this a false alarm?
A figment of my over-active mind?
Not quite.
This day is a reprieve.
The patient rallies –
But not for long.

The greens will turn to red and gold and brown
And spiral to the ground.
The season in a minor key returns
To toughen me against the
Winter yet to come.

If all the seasons sang a jubilant song,
How would I recognize the rhapsody of spring?

32

Reading Matters

The first *Life Support* piece I wrote for the *Pittsburgh Post-Gazette,* "A Reader's Dilemma," which appears earlier in this book, expressed my frustration at not having time to read everything I'd like to read. And in the intervening years the situation has only gotten worse. Back then I had not yet come under the spell of Amazon.com and its "Wish List" and "Save for Later" blandishments. And although some fear that the reading of books might be a dying pastime, I see no sign of this as bookstores become more elaborate, everybody and his brother is writing a book, and electronic readers are selling by the truckload.

Me, I'm old-fashioned. I want to *hold* my book and keep a bookmark in it to see how far along I am. I want to flip back through the pages to read snippets to my husband, make notes in the margins, and jot down unfamiliar words inside the back flyleaf. And once I've started a book, unless it's a real stinker, I want to see it through to its ending, bitter or not. I have a nagging fear that if I owned an electronic reader I'd read a few pages, think, "This isn't for me," download another title, have the same reaction, and who knows? – sample book after book until I had exhausted the entire Western canon.

Whatever book I'm reading is usually relegated to the few minutes before I nod off at night, because the daytime is taken up with reading the morning paper and the clusters of periodicals that fill our mailbox. I was keeping up pretty well until we were given a gift subscription to *The New Yorker*. Then the situation went from being frustrating to downright dire. *The New Yorker* is a daunting publication because the articles are so long. In the doctor's office I could get away with just scanning the cartoons before my name was called. But now that it comes into our home, I feel a certain responsibility to *read* it. So I drag it around with the others, stealing time from changing the sheets or watching *Dog the Bounty Hunter*, to give it its due.

My taste in books is nothing if not eclectic. Although I lean towards non-fiction, I've read everything from *Enter Whining*, the autobiography of Fran Drescher, to *The Magic Mountain* by Thomas Mann, translated from the German and considered one of the most influential works of twentieth century literature.

Along with my frantic efforts to keep up with the magazines, I have actually managed to read several books from cover to cover during 2010. And, as the season of gift-giving closes in on us, for the readers on your list I offer these recommendations (in alphabetical order):

The Bean Trees by Barbara Kingsolver, who also wrote *The Poisonwood Bible*. I *loved* this novel about a young woman who is suddenly faced with an unexpected responsibility. Even though it might fit into the Young Adult category, this "seasoned citizen" enjoyed its charms immensely.

The Book Thief by Markus Zusak employs Death as its narrator. The time is 1939, and the main characters are a young German girl and her family, who are hiding a Jewish man in the basement. Don't be put off by the grim description. This is an extraordinary work that everyone who appreciates great writing should read or at least know about.

Hitch 22 by Christopher Hitchens is the memoir of this controversial British-American journalist/intellectual. Whoever reads it will up his or her IQ by a few points and enjoy it in the bargain.

My Times in Black and White: Race and Power at the New York Times by Gerald R. Boyd. If you were at all interested in the Jason Blair plagiarism scandal, that painful episode is detailed blow by painful blow by former managing editor Boyd whose head was one of those that rolled in the wake of the upheaval. *My Times* is a primer on how stressful life can be in the offices of "the newspaper of record." Writing for *The New York Times* is not for the faint of heart.

Not Entitled is a memoir by Sir Frank Kermode, who died in August of this year. Born in 1919 on the Isle of Man, Kermode became a foremost literary critic and theorist. *Time* magazine's description of *Not Entitled* as "wry" and "quizzical" intrigued me enough to order the book, and I wasn't disappointed as I read about Kermode's youthful deprivation, his time in the Royal Navy, and his turbulent academic life. And it was comforting to know that despite his towering intellect and impeccable credentials, Kermode, like many of us, was tormented with self-doubt.

Running with Scissors by Augusten Burroughs is an autobiography, although it's hard to believe that some of the bizarre events he describes really occurred. *Running with Scissors* is not for the prudish or squeamish, but it is guaranteed to keep you thinking "Merciful heavens!" as you turn the pages. Made into a movie with an excellent cast – Annette Bening, Jill Clayburgh, Gwyneth Paltrow – it is worth watching just to see how a few of the episodes described in the book are recreated on the screen.

The Tower, the Zoo, and the Tortoise by Julia Stuart is a darkly whimsical tale about a Beefeater at the Tower of London, his wife, and an odd assortment of characters – and critters. If dark whimsy is your cup of tea, this one fits the bill.

Never say never. A year after I wrote this piece I became an iPad owner and, as of April 2013, have read thirty-five books on it and have delighted in the convenience and easy access. I cannot imagine returning to hardcover books unless there's no e-Reader version available.

2011

33

January 2011

The Virtue Fund

One day several years ago, on the way home from a morning rehearsal, I decided to stop at a Chinese restaurant in a neighborhood along the way to pick up some take-out for lunch. But the closer I got to the restaurant the less I felt like looking for a parking space and waiting for my order. Instead, I thought, I'll go straight home, make myself a tuna salad sandwich, and put the money I would have spent into an envelope. That was the beginning of what I later dubbed the Virtue Fund. I wrote Virtue Fund on the envelope and drew a little stick figure wearing a skirt and a halo.

From then on, whenever I didn't spend an amount of money that I had expected to spend, I would put it into the Virtue Fund, and eventually I accumulated a tidy sum.

For years, we've been hearing that the best way to become financially secure is to pay ourselves first. Many of us have money deducted from our pay, before we can get our hands on it, which goes into an IRA or other type of investment account. An old-fashioned but tried and true way is to deposit a set amount each week or month into a savings account – sort of like tithing, but to our futures or a trip to the Caribbean instead of to our place of worship. The trick, of course, is to *do* it, not to fall off the wagon and raid the account at the least little bump in the road.

I abandoned the Virtue Fund for a while but recently took it up again. For years I did my own hair – at least the shampoo and curl part. Then I decided to be profligate and have it done professionally every week, convinced that I had worked hard and deserved the indulgence.

But on a recent cruise of the Amazon, there wasn't a beauty salon on the boat or for hundreds of miles in any direction. I realized that if my hair was to be done I would have to do it myself, and it came out just fine – better actually than when done by the local stylist who insists on sending me away with a helmet head.

I wasn't completely cured of my free-spending habit. After all, what is more relaxing than to plant yourself in a salon chair and read a book while somebody else does the work? But in the name of virtue, I decided to tackle the job again. And when I finished, I put twenty-eight dollars into an envelope. This was the beginning of the *new* Virtue Fund.

A week later another twenty-eight dollars went into the envelope. And then – and you'll agree that I was getting brave – I decided to touch up the barely visible gray roots at my temples. I bought some touch-up color, brought it home and discovered to my dismay that I first had to perform a forty-eight hour allergy test. Darn. That delay and increasing anxiety about how it might turn out were almost enough to change my mind. But a neighbor encouraged me to do it, I did it, and the results were spot on. And into the Virtue Fund went thirty-five dollars. However, there is one thing I am *not* virtuous enough to do – cut my own hair. When I try that, anyone who sees me will know I've become a little too thrifty.

The other day my husband figured out how to keep the kitchen faucet from dripping. Sixty-four dollars – what the plumber would have charged – went into the Virtue Fund. So, with just a little effort, there's already a nice little stash. For a new barbecue grill? For a trip to Disney World?

What you do with your Virtue Fund is up to you, and getting there is not only painless, but the minimal effort you expend is more than made up for by a feeling of – virtue.

There's bound to be something you spend money on that you could do without or do for yourself. I don't know what it is, but you do. Maybe it's a service, or perhaps you could dine out one less night a week. Or bring home prepared food from the supermarket and put the difference between what it would have cost in a restaurant, along with the tip, into the Virtue Fund.

Are you a coupon clipper? Save three dollars? Put three dollars into the fund. If you find a free or metered parking space instead of having to go into an expensive garage, put the savings into the Virtue Fund. Are you a reader? Check to see which books on your wish list are available from the library and put the book money into the fund. You'll be amazed at how fast it accumulates and how easy it is. Just don't make the mistake of mixing up your Virtue Fund money with any other money so that you lose track of your accomplishment.

Many Americans seem to have abandoned the habit of saving for a rainy day. That's a concept from a bygone era. But recent statistics show that the Chinese, who are gaining on us in myriad ways, save twenty percent of what they earn. Americans save five percent. And frankly, I'm surprised we save that much. We love to spend, spend, spend, or should I say charge, charge, charge, and worry later about where the money will come from. Too many of us feel we should be able to live like rich people, and the result is that we keep battalions of credit counselors, some of whom are on the shady side, busy, and prosperous.

So it might not be a bad idea, at the beginning of a new year, to start a *new* old fashion and save up for a few things *before* we buy them. Virtue is defined as "a characteristic valued for promoting individual and collective well being," and what better way to enjoy a feeling of well being than to have a little nest egg hidden away for a rainy day, or a day at the beach – in the Caribbean?

34

February 2011

Are They Killing Us?

Have you ever brought home the remainder of your restaurant entree and been aghast when, after it has spent the night in your refrigerator, the whole business comes out of the container in a lump? The lovely *sauce* that coated your chicken or shrimp has hardened into mostly butter.

Chefs are busy people who know that nothing tastes as good as real butter, and they toss it around the kitchen with little regard for how it will affect the individual diner. The chef doesn't give a hoot about the dimensions of your hips or the level of your triglycerides.

And in case you think this is typical of only chain restaurants, think again. I ordered a lovely chicken dish with tagliolini pasta, grilled baby squash, capers, herbs, arugula, and *pan jus* at a fairly upscale restaurant. The *pan jus* was mostly oil. And although it was delicious, I felt as if I was eating melted butter with a spoon; with every bite I contemplated how I would deprive myself of anything edible for the next few days.

When I was growing up in the Dark Ages, after World War II, we ate in moderation, and we dined in restaurants only on special occasions, if at all. And the neighborhood grocery store carried one or two kinds of potato chips, not two aisles filled with every kind of high sodium, carb-loaded snack imaginable.

But somewhere along the line it was decided that, when it comes to food, the more the merrier, the bigger the better. Cookies and muffins used to be two or three inches in diameter. Now we can buy cookies and muffins the size of compact discs. And why should we settle for grandma's puny nine-inch apple pie when we can go to the nearby warehouse store and get an eye-popping twelve-inch version?

Our world of abundance is now arranged so that in case there isn't a supermarket within five hundred yards, we can buy edibles in office supply stores, at department store entryways where chocolate bars are on display, and of course at the ubiquitous convenience store. So we never again need worry about moving more than a few feet to the left or right without something to eat being within reach.

Eating has become a religion. Our lives are organized around eating so that not long after breakfast we start meditating on what might taste good for lunch. And if we want to hold a meeting, it's a good bet that people will show up if food is involved. Drinks and snacks not on the agenda? Attendance will be sparse.

In case football and hockey aren't enough spectator sports to satisfy you, there is a sport that has been taking off in a big way – the eating contest. What a great idea! Could there be a more noble distinction than to be the person who can eat the most hamburgers, hot dogs, chicken wings, or pancakes? Could there be a better role model for our kids who are already bursting out of their jeans?

The average woman, to maintain her weight, should consume around 2000 calories a day. So let's take her out to dinner at a popular chain restaurant. Maybe she'll order the Beer-battered Fish and Chips, a small Caesar Salad, and the Wild Blueberry and White Chocolate Cheesecake for dessert. She'll probably have a little garlic toast and a beverage or two. The fish and chips are 1832 calories and, by the way, contain 3232 milligrams of sodium, more than twice the recommended amount for an entire day. The salad is 860 calories – yes, a little Caesar side salad – and the cheesecake is 929. Without beverages and bread the meal totals a staggering 3621 calories. And there are people who eat like that every day.

To be fair, many menus do have a few low-calorie or heart-healthy choices. But when those French fries are calling your name or a slice of whipped-cream topped devil's food cake sails past your table, how much self-discipline can you be expected to have?

When it comes to eating too much of the wrong thing, most of the blame should be placed on what I like to call "Big Food," the food industry that, with utter disregard for the consequences, will do whatever it takes to get us to eat way more than we should. They know that Americans have little self-control when it comes to eating and even less intention of saying no to themselves about anything else.

But in truth, they're not forcing food down our throats. We're doing it to ourselves, bite by bite, gulp by gulp. And I'm as vulnerable as the next person to the lure of the mid-evening pizza commercials or the all-you-can-eat buffet.

But we must at least try to get a grip on our compulsion to eat. There's a poem by William Ernest Henley titled "Invictus," undefeated, that we might keep in mind. The final lines read, "I am the master of my fate / I am the captain of my soul."

Perhaps we can give a little more thought to becoming the captains of our appetites if we bring home two-thirds of that restaurant meal to nibble on for several days and, for heaven's sake, stay out of eating contests.

35

They Can *Take That Away From Me*

And they have.

How often have you tried to purchase a product you've been using for years only to find that it's been discontinued? You experience a combination of disappointment and anxiety. Items you've become used to are supposed to be available forever – or at least until you discover something you like better.

My list of discontinued products is growing apace, but there's a glimmer of hope albeit fading. At one time, if you could no longer find your favorite product in a store, you were out of luck. Now, with the help of the Internet and Google searches, some of those tried-and-true items are still available. They'll cost us more because of shipping charges, but if we really want them we're willing to pay a few extra bucks.

For many years I used Baggies brand plastic bags, the ones in the red box with the green alligator logo that comes with a supply of twist ties. I kept a supply of the one- and two-gallon sizes for a couple of decades until one day, when I looked for them on the supermarket shelves, they had disappeared.

How could I go on without my beloved Baggies? How would I store the Thanksgiving turkey carcass until

I had time to remove the meat for soup? How else does one store a turkey carcass? Ziploc bags are good for a lot of things but it's not easy to find a Ziploc-type bag that is roomy enough for a turkey carcass.

When I had given up hope a catalog arrived from the mail order company Home Trends, and to my delight they carry Baggies. I'm not sure why they happen to have a supply of Baggies when no one else does, but I'm happy they do, and I order several boxes at a time – the heck with the shipping charges – so that I'll have a supply in case theirs runs out.

I've had the same success purchasing a few other products via the Internet including Texize K2R Spot Lifter and Cover Girl Trublend whipped makeup.

My luck hasn't been so good with a couple of my favorite unmentionables. The undies I wore for years are absolutely not available anywhere, not even on eBay or gently worn. Ugh. And the other undie, the bra that hooks in the front, has disappeared, never to return.

Why did they discontinue the hair texurizer that had been the answer to my humid weather prayers? I found all that remained on Planet Earth – no joke – twelve treatments, and bought it from a company in California that was closing out the brand. My supply is dwindling and I'm praying that a mad scientist somewhere is cooking up a formula that will work as well.

The handle came off my husband's favorite knife, the one he uses to slice onions and carrots for salad. Internet search? No dice. We've spent a small fortune on knives that he might like as well, but so far *not* so good.

Perhaps a downside to living too long is that they keep taking stuff away from us. Demographic changes play into the mix, plus, the stores are so crammed with new and improved merchandise that they have to get rid of the old to free up space.

That said, if you're in danger of suffering withdrawal symptoms, my advice is this: If there's something you can't get along without, stock up on it now because, when that great *they* out there in the world of retail gets wind that you've come to depend on it, quick as a wink they'll take it off the market.

36

The Help

Having recently read a book that has become a word-of-mouth phenomenon, *The Help* by Kathryn Stockett, I'm going to assume that you have, too.

Resistant to popular best-sellers, I was a holdout. I didn't think it would break any new ground for me to read a fictionalized account of the way white housewives in Mississippi mistreated their black maids in the 1960s. Most of us are aware of how disgracefully black people have been treated in this country until relatively recently.

But so many people asked me if I had read it that I finally succumbed. I bought a hardcover copy – still the only version available of a book, which, at this writing, has been on *The New York Times* best-seller list for more than a hundred weeks – sixty weeks longer than its closest runner-up, *The Girl Who Kicked the Hornet's Nest*, the third of the Stieg Larsen trilogy of thrillers starring the cunning Liz Salander who takes on her tormentors and crushes them. They pay for their atrocities and we cheer.

The Help is its own kind of thriller, a domestic thriller. It is suspenseful. Jobs, marriages, friendships, and even lives are at stake. And the courageous Skeeter, like so many brave souls before and after who have attempted to shine a light on injustice, risks everything to get the maids' stories told.

Even so, I'm amazed that it has been such a monster hit. Exactly what is it that all of these readers, mostly women, find so compelling? *The Help* is a well-told story. But how many well-told stories are published every day that gather dust in book stores before being remaindered to discount book stores or sent to the pulping machines?

Is it simply a twist of fate? Stockett began writing *The Help* in her New York City office soon after 9/11 when her hard drive was destroyed and she couldn't even make a phone call. All that was left to her was pen, paper, and memories. And what started out to be a short story about events of her youth blossomed into a full-length novel. It was shunned by publishers. Stockett stopped counting rejections at forty-five before Susan Ramer at Putnam sensed that there was something extraordinary on those pages.

Perhaps *The Help* hits a nerve not only because it's about the subjugation of black women, but because it speaks to the subjugation of women in general. The housewives of *The Help* subjugated their household help, treating them as inferiors according to the culture of the day. But those ladies of the house were themselves subjugated by the culture. Although affluent and cherished, they had little power outside of their own homes. Besides their children, over whom did they have any real power? Only their domestic help. And they wielded it in demeaning ways. A separate toilet in the garage for the maid? That seems outrageous to us now, but that's how things were not so long ago.

It will soon be fifty years since Betty Freidan's world-altering study of American women, *The Feminine Mystique, was* published, also after many rejections. It is interesting to reflect on what women's lives were like in the early sixties compared with what they are like today. Occupations open to women were limited to a degree hard to believe in the twenty-first century. You could be a school teacher, or you could be a secretary at a place like *Mad Men*'s Sterling Cooper advertising agency. You could work for the government or in retailing.

In the early sixties, ninety-seven percent of doctors were men. Ninety-seven percent of lawyers were men, as were political officials. Male-only institutions such as the National Press Club allowed female reporters to sit only in the balcony, and they were not permitted to ask questions. Forget about female CEOs or Supreme Court justices. So many occupations where we now see women without giving it much thought just didn't exist in 1963. There were no female bus drivers, mail carriers, or police officers. Opportunities for ordinary women to make a decent living were limited.

And the inequities didn't end there. I was stunned, in the early 1970s, when I had been working for the Pittsburgh Symphony for several years, to learn that if I wanted my own credit card the application would have to be signed by my soon-to-be ex-husband who, at the time, was a graduate student at the University of Pittsburgh and didn't have a job.

Evelyn Bitner Pearson, in her *Portrait of a Pittsburgh Family,* relates that when she was ready to divorce her unproductive husband, she was informed that her stock certificates, which were the product of her father's wealth, were to be turned over to her husband. Department stores suddenly denied her credit and she had to hire a lawyer in order to get a mortgage.

Even in 2011 we know that women are still, in many ways, objects of ridicule and chauvinism. Despite equal opportunity and workplace harassment laws, many woman, especially those in non-traditional jobs, are still working in a *Mad Men* environment where a too-tight squeeze or fanny pat must be suffered in silence.

Perhaps I'm barking up the wrong tree in making a connection between the issues raised in *The Help* and the struggles of women in general. But although I'm not a bra-burning feminist I do believe that women, black women in particular, still have a lot of scores to settle before they achieve equity and equality, even in the twenty-first century.

37

Write It Down

When I retired a few years ago it seemed like it might be a good idea to put down some memoirs. By then I had lived a fairly long and interesting life. I typed reminiscences into my computer for a while but eventually fell away from it. Everything else I was doing at the computer – answering emails, shopping online, watching the YouTube videos that arrive in batches – gave me an excuse to procrastinate. With so many things taking precedence, the memoir file lay dormant for several years until a few weeks ago.

A writer/historian was recently in town doing research at the University of Pittsburgh archives on my father, P. L. Prattis, who was editor of the *Pittsburgh* Courier, and whose career was significant enough for his obituary to appear in the *New York Times* on March 3, 1980.

Unearthing details about this man, gone for thirty years, is not easy because, although my father left behind a small mountain of documents, he left very little autobiographical information. Hardly anything is known about his childhood up until around age fourteen, when he was sent off to school by a kindly Quaker lady. And because he was an only child and father of an only child, there is no succession of nieces, nephews, or grandchildren to help stitch together his story.

Having never written anything longer than a few pages, I suspect that what had been holding me back was that I lacked a plan of how to document nearly seven decades of living. I had been dumping information into the "My Life" file without a blueprint.

I toyed with the idea of putting each topic on an index card, but I figured that the cards would become yet another jumble of disorganization.

Then one day a light went on inside my head. Now this might seem like the most obvious and fundamental step in writing one's biography, but it just hadn't occurred to me: Write an outline.

I sketched an outline, in chronological order, and it's been smoother sailing ever since. Topics are inserted where they belong, or at least where they *might* belong. And I can insert forgotten incidents that bubble to the surface.

I haven't forgotten as much as I thought I had. This process is bringing into focus fuzzy memories that I thought were lost forever. And I'm realizing, for good or ill, how much my personality and habits resemble those of my parents.

All of this underscores how important it is for us to write about our lives, because one day somebody might just want to know what we did and what made us tick. And nobody knows that better than we do.

In recently reading *Chronicle of a Pittsburgh Family* by Evelyn Bitner Pearson, who was born on June 20, 1910, two days before my mother, I learned that Pearson's father, Harry Murray Bitner, was the editor of the *Pittsburgh Press* before Scripps Howard bought it and later the publisher of the *Pittsburgh Sun-Telegraph*. And he was a high ranking executive in the Hearst Corporation. It is interesting to read the history of that family, where they came from and how they happened to settle in Pittsburgh. But it's even more interesting to read about the mundane things of everyday life – the ice man, the scissors grinder, the sad irons that housewives used to iron their husband's stiffly starched shirts in the early 1900s.

What was life like during your childhood? What appliances were in use? Who were your neighbors? What did you do for fun before computers and video games? Were you ever beaten up? I was. Did you ever beat up anybody? I didn't.

Mrs. Pearson led an interesting life, but so have you. So get busy. You have a story to tell, and it's important to tell it before, somewhere down the line, somebody else tries to tell it – and gets it wrong.

They say that well-begun is half-done. And I can confidently say that I'm well-begun. If I write for fifteen minutes a day for the next year, it will amount to ninety-one hours. Not even *my* utterly fascinating life story should take longer than that.

38

Food Then, Food Now

The first time I tasted a taco was in Los Angeles, in 1959. I went there to participate as winner of a local Shriner's beauty and talent pageant and enjoyed the bonus of staying with relatives for a week afterwards. One evening my uncle took us out for tacos. I had never tasted a taco, and it was love at first bite. And I begged my uncle to take us there every evening for the rest of my stay. I was smitten. The taco was the first international food I had ever tasted, unless you want to include in that category La Choy chow mein or Chef Boyardee spaghetti and meatballs. *Al dente, al shmente.*

How the world of food has changed. Most of us grew up in homes where the fare was pretty prosaic: Meatloaf and mashed potatoes, fried chicken, macaroni and cheese, pork chops, spaghetti and meatballs, and mushy peas and green beans, mostly canned. In our house, we regularly dined on stewed chicken – prepared in the Presto pressure cooker, wieners and beans, occasionally corned beef and cabbage, or ham hocks and black-eyed peas. My mother, a Pittsburgh native, wasn't especially interested in preparing black-eyed peas, but she fixed them for my father. Even though he was a Philadelphian, he liked a taste of soul food now and then.

When we were young did fish come in any other form than frozen in foot-long boxes – haddock, perch, and sole – or in cans? There was no such thing as fresh salmon, or tuna, or trout. And there certainly was no shrimp around. I'm not sure how old I was before I ever saw a real shrimp, in a shell. Clams and oysters came smoked in cans you had to open with a key. It was fun removing the key and coiling the metal strip around the can until, voilà, the lid popped off. If we wanted a salad, we bought a head of lettuce, iceberg lettuce. What other kind was there?

That was then. This is now. A visit to a modern supermarket, especially the produce department, is like a visit to an international bazaar. We have become accustomed to seeing snow peas and ginger root, bok choy and tofu. We recognize jalapenos and tomatillos, romaine and radicchio, spring mix and broccolini. We can choose from four different colors of bell peppers, yellow and orange tomatoes, and white and purple asparagus. But we're still a little dubious about fussy salad greens such as mesclun and mâche and frisée. And in the not-too-distant past, we didn't know a leek from a fennel and considered a scallion a bit suspect.

Today's abundance and variety of foods is staggering. If you took your grandmother through the Market District or Whole Foods, you'd better take along the smelling salts, because she would keel over from sensual and visual overload. As it is, I sometimes think I may collapse from overstimulation.

Everyday food in the fifties and sixties is what we now call comfort food, perhaps to distinguish it from much of what we eat now, which might be thought of as anxiety food. It makes us a little nervous. We don't always know what it is, how to pronounce it, or how to cook it, and we worry about what our family or company might think if we serve it to them.

And some of the hip, new restaurant menus can be a source of anxiety. There's a new, cutting-edge place in town whose menu scares the socks off some first-time diners who are confronted, before they drift down the page to familiar-sounding salads and entrees, by three lists of items in a kind of "One from Column A, one from Column B" arrangement. Many of the offerings – meats and cheeses – are unfamiliar except to genuine foodies. Do you know what Finnochiona, Cypress Midnight Moon and Quince Mostarda are? If you do, you're ahead of me, and if you don't, they are a meat, a cheese, and a fruit condiment.

Our culinary revolution is the result of two factors: travel and immigration. The world has, in fact, become small. We swipe our credit cards, jet off to destinations only dreamed of in our youth, and our culinary world expands. And as we fly across great bodies of water, others cross into our country bringing with them a world of new flavors and textures. When I was a young woman it would have been difficult to imagine a Thai or Korean restaurant in Pittsburgh. Vietnamese? Heavens, most of us had never heard of Vietnam until it came crashing into our living rooms on the evening news. Now, there are at least ten Vietnamese restaurants within easy driving distance.

European cuisine, from which came our menu until the mid-twentieth century, has been left on the back burner as we've become familiar with sushi and pad thai, hummus and couscous, curry and gazpacho.

But, despite these revolutionary offerings, despite our growing sophistication and the profusion of choices, what would you imagine still to be the most popular food in the world? Certainly French fries and burgers are beloved everywhere, but I believe the hands down winner is pizza.

You cannot travel anywhere without finding some variation of it, whether it's called pizza or flatbread, deep-dish or thin-crust, round or rectangular. And it is available topped with just about everything but marinated bumblebees, which should be coming soon to a pizzeria near you.

39

Passwords

There's not much in this world that makes me want to hurl my computer out the window more than passwords.

Since 1995, when I got my first computer, I've thought up a thousand different passwords, at least it seems like that many. Obviously, I believe that the passwords I come up with are good ones, obscure enough not to be figured out by anyone. Yet when I sign on to a new site and am asked for a password, nearly every one I enter, no matter how foolproof it seems to me, is rejected as "weak." How in the world could *enyefyg3* be weak? I jest. I haven't tried that one, but maybe I will.

One of my passwords contains thirteen letters. So, although it's usually accepted, I'm not real keen to have to enter half the alphabet to get to my Delta SkyMiles account.

Perhaps most annoying is being told to reset my password, which means that I cannot reuse the password I've been using for years. I must modify it in some way – add another letter or a couple of numbers. And often, while I'm thrashing around trying to find something that works, there appears the cheery question, "Forgot password?" - sort of like, "Got milk?" Of *course* I've forgotten the bloody password or I wouldn't be sitting here

171

wasting time that I'll never get back trying to get to my blankety-blank credit card statement.

A recent episode involved accessing my Citizens Bank account. The password stored on my two-page and growing list of passwords suddenly wouldn't work. So the tormentor behind the screen tried another tack, a security question. Where was my father born? That's easy. Philadelphia. Wouldn't accept Philadelphia. Then I was asked my mother's middle name. I typed that in and again, nada. Eventually, I found out that I had originally typed in Philadelphia *PA*. Not sure why I did that. Is there more than one Philadelphia? Maybe they asked for the state abbreviation to be included. By then I hadn't the slightest idea.

For years, I've easily gotten into our investment account to see what kind of damage the stock market has done to our nest egg. Then one day I click the link in Favorites and get the following message: "We're sorry, the page you have requested is not available. If you typed in the address, check to make sure you entered it correctly." Hmph. The strange thing about that is that at the top of the page there's a bar that says, "Portfolios and Accounts." I clicked on it and, presto! – in I went.

We've been made to feel that we have to conduct all of these business transactions online because the retailers and financial institutions just about come right out and tell us, point blank, that they *do not wish* to speak to us by phone. They try to convince us that we'd be much happier visiting their convenient website. But of course, the truth is that they don't want to talk to us because talking to us costs them money. The real message is, "Get lost."

An envelope from the Social Security Administration arrived today that announced: "Your temporary Password request Code (PRC) is: 123456." (I do not remember requesting a temporary Password request Code, but maybe I did.) It goes on to say, "This is not a password. Use it to create a permanent password before April 17." So, in essence, I'm being given a password to create – a password.

A tech-savvy friend insisted that she had the answer to my woes via a site called Splash.com that would store all of my passwords, serial numbers, bra size, everything. The fact that I already had my passwords stored on my computer didn't satisfy her. So I took the bait, went to the site and, for ten bucks, signed up, whereupon I was immediately thrown into password purgatory. In a state of paralyzing anxiety, I logged off and decided that my ten dollars to Splash.com would make a contribution to their favorite charity.

The problem with all of these passwords, of course, is that only a wizard could remember all of them, es-pecially in their constantly changing configurations. Maybe we should ditch the whole lot, go back to cave-man days, and start all over again. Caveman talk might work well as passwords – grunt, phhtt, glerg.

As we acquire more devices and more apps, things are only going to get worse. I just hope that the uber-smart people who have brought us touch screen just-about-everything will figure out a way that we can be identified by the feel of our fingertip, the hue of our eyeball, or a little puff of our smokin' hot breath. All of those identifiers should be like fingerprints or DNA: no two alike.

Maybe there's an app for that.

40

Letters

During the past few weeks, I've been going through boxes and bags of letters that have been stored in our basement since my mother passed away in 2005. My mother saved *everything,* and there are hundreds of letters written to me by the individuals who peopled my life in my youth. Sorry to say, a few of those letters are from people I no longer remember even with the help of a return address on the envelope. And there are missives from young men that I didn't have sense enough to realize – or wouldn't acknowledge – had more than a platonic interest in me. There were hints of wishful thinking between the lines.

Some of the letters were from friends who wrote at my father's urging when I was away at music camp or traveling overseas with the orchestra, and I appreciate those handwritten accounts of the hometown comings and goings even more in retrospect.

Handwritten letters have always been special, and they are becoming more so as their frequency diminishes. They are written by the computer-averse, people like my husband, who refuse to become involved with technology. Some are written by friends whose computers are out of commission. I recently received a long letter from a cousin in Ohio who wrote it by hand because her house had gone up in flames, and with it her computer.

Spared from the blaze was a sheaf of letters written to her mother, my aunt, by my mother, beginning in 1927, when she was a junior at Langley High School. It is difficult for us to imagine our parents as young people. And although I knew that as one of four orphaned siblings, raised by relatives, she had had a difficult youth, I was nevertheless taken aback to see the accounts, in black and white, of the daily struggles that she confided to her sister.

As she approached her thirties, she was still single and afraid that life had passed her by. But her fortunes changed. She wrote to her sister: "I received a letter the other day from a man at work. He is an editor and about forty years old. He has always liked me, but I didn't know how much until his wife left him a couple of months ago." Oooh – what a juicy tidbit. That letter writer was my father.

Their courtship flourished, much of it by letter, until they married in 1939. My father's early advances were typed, on letterhead stationery, which I found sweetly amusing. However, as he became more sure of himself and his sentiments more ardent, a change was made to hand-written *billets-doux*.

Traditionally, letters and diaries document much of our history. For hundreds of years, letters have shone a light onto the personal lives of those who came before. Entire collections of letters have themselves become classics.

And now we have Facebook and Twitter.

A hundred years from now will researchers be reading Facebook updates and tweets from 2011? Without the personal letter to rely on, by what means will students of history come to know how we felt about our lives? Will any account be permanent?

Much electronic correspondence can be saved and retrieved, so perhaps the budding romance of Prince William and Kate, in a series of tweets and text messages, will be easily accessed by romantics and historians of the twenty-second century. But how romantic will they seem compared to the tenderly wrought sentiments of Elizabeth Barrett to Robert Browning: "How do I love thee? Let me count the ways."

I would never have imagined that the handwritten letter would become as quaint and obsolete as the payphone and the full-service gas station. But that day is close at hand, and with it a move afoot to eliminate the teaching of cursive writing from school curricula. Maybe that's not the worst thing that could happen in this world, but I somehow feel that we are losing something precious and uniquely personal.

41

QWERTY

"It makes no sense. It is awkward, inefficient and confusing. We've been saying that for 124 years. But there it remains, the rickety, clumsy device marketed as the 'Type-Writer' in 1872, whose arrangement of letters has remained the standard on even the most advanced, sophisticated computers and word processors electronic technology can produce." That was written by Darryl Rehr, editor of the *Journal of the Early Typewriter*, describing the QWERTY keyboard, the one we use every day.

Other than the ability to play the piano, there is no skill I treasure more than my ability to type. My mother taught me to type, using the bona fide touch system, when I was twelve. I thought it was fun but didn't appreciate what a valuable lifelong skill I was acquiring.

The clackety old Underwood in our house eventually got itself traded in for a sky blue Olivetti, which must have seemed outrageous at the time, just as when somebody decided that all cars didn't have to be black.

A few years later, when she was in an extravagant mood, my mother bought a reconditioned IBM Selectric, the one whose letters were on a rotating ball instead of at the ends of individual levers. That revolutionary development might have justified the fact that the machine weighed just under a ton. Actually, it weighed thirty pounds, but when we had to lug it to another room, it felt like a ton.

After hours of practicing "The quick brown fox jumps over the lazy dog" I began to acquire speed and precision. By my mid-teens, I typed well enough to do fill-in work during the summer in the office of the *Pittsburgh Courier* where my father worked. One of my jobs was typing letters for him. And I laugh now to recall how many copies I had to type before I came up with one neat enough to present for his signature.

Back then, when we made a typing mistake, before the appearance of Wite-Out, we used what were called *pencil erasers*. They looked like pencils but had a sharpened eraser on one end and a brush on the other. And an over-zealous attempt to erase a mistake could result in an unsightly hole in the paper.

During World War I, when the higher-ups discovered that my father could type, he was put to work in an office and spared going into battle. And although he wrote for newspapers for more than forty years, he never learned the touch system. His typing was of the two-fingered, hunt and peck variety. His typing kept him from going into battle although he could never have qualified to be a contestant in the National Typing Bee.

I wouldn't qualify for that charmed circle either, but I am capable of typing at great speed. When my non-typing husband presented me with a document to transcribe recently, as my fingers tore around the keyboard, he remarked, "I don't know how you *do* that." He's been *hearing* me do it for years, when he's sitting in the next room, but he was amazed by it as he stood next to me.

That got me thinking about how those of us who are decent typists have managed to master such a queer and illogical arrangement of letters. The keyboard we use is called the QWERTY keyboard because that's what the top row of letters begins with. This arrangement was developed in the 1860s by Christopher Latham Sholes, a newspaper man in Milwaukee, when the typesetters went on strike. And since then the evolution of the typewriter has brought us a plethora of bizarre-looking contraptions.

Sholes and his partners were granted patents for their invention in 1868. After much experimentation, the QWERTY configuration was the only one that didn't cause the levers to which the letters were attached to become tangled and jam the machines. And although there have been many tinkerers over the years who have thought they had come up with a better system, little headway has been made in a country where QWERTY has become the undisputed standard.

We are so used to it that the very idea of a different arrangement makes us a little nervous. The letters on my portable GPS device are arranged alphabetically. One might expect that to be simple enough, but with the letters not in the QWERTY configuration, I have to *think* about where to go next.

I have had occasion to type on keyboards in foreign countries. Because some letters are used differently or not at all, it is impossible not to become confused. On a French keyboard, the A is where the Q is on our keyboards. So it is necessary to check every line to change words such as *zuick* to *quick* and *qpple* to *apple.* Nearly every language has its own keyboard idiosyncrasies. Even the British keyboard is different from ours; it contains the symbols for the pound (£) and the euro (€).

Until computers came into general use, keyboards were used primarily by secretaries and those who wrote for a living. Now, with the widespread use of the computer, recent generations have discovered, to their dismay, that they lack a much-needed skill. And I don't envy them. Most middle and high school students are now required to take a course in keyboarding. And it's a good thing because learning to type is like learning to play the piano or speak a foreign language – best done in one's youth. And it's a testament to the flexibility of the human brain that it can process a system that made sense to the developers but appears to us to be so utterly random.

42

The Weather

What is more useless than talking about the weather? Not much, except, if you can't think of anything else to say to a stranger in an elevator or while waiting for a bus you can always fill the silence by commenting on the weather.

I avoid writing about the weather because it's bound to devolve into complaining or speculating. But now that we've safely made it to August I thought I'd make a few remarks about the environment in which we find ourselves.

My husband and I like to go to a warm climate in February or early March, usually on a cruise. Struggling through the dank chill of December and January, we in the temperate zone figure that if we put off a winter getaway until mid-February, winter will be over by the time we get back a few weeks later. Think again.

In March it snowed. It plummeted into the teens. It hailed. It played tricks on us. When the weatherman announced that March 21st would be arriving the following Monday, we thought, "Oh boy, spring will be here soon!"

But, again, we were deluding ourselves. Heading towards April there was more snow to come, more sub-freezing temperatures and the teeth-rattling March winds. And when it was over, what did we have to show for? A yard full of twigs and split trees with dispirited limbs hanging from their trunks. There was no sign of spring.

When it poured in April we comforted ourselves with the reminder that "April showers bring May flowers." But it rained so much in May that about all we could do was stand in the house, peering through rain-streaked windows, as optimistic buds struggled to burst forth. And we wondered if we would ever be able to bring out the patio furniture and put away the space heaters.

Grumble though we may, considering what has happened in the rest of the world since the beginning of the year, we in Western Pennsylvania should reconsider complaining about the weather. If we can abandon for a moment our "grass is always greener" reflex, we have to agree that we are among the luckiest people in the United States. There aren't many areas of the country that have been spared weather resulting in catastrophic loss of life and property.

I'm not a meteorologist, but I theorize that Pittsburgh is protected by its topography – its hills and valleys – from all but the most determined weather disasters. Perhaps it's only a matter of time, but so far we haven't been targeted by earthquakes and tsunamis, hurricanes and floods, volcanoes, wildfires, landslides, dust storms, ice storms, and life-threatening heat waves. The last tornado that hit Pittsburgh was thirteen years ago and was minor compared to those in Joplin, Missouri, and other Midwest towns where five-hundred thirty-six lives have been lost this year.

As we watch the evening news with feelings of "There but for the grace of God…" we experience a twinge of survivor's guilt and aren't quite as confident as we have been that our luck will hold out.

What is happening? Is it global warming? Coincidence? Just like any other year except that our memories are short? Perhaps the Reverend Harold Camping, our foremost predictor of doom, is right about the world coming to an end, except that instead of happening all at once, it's arriving in installments.

All of this makes one wonder if mankind was supposed to advance to the degree he has, to dwell in multi-level structures overflowing with earthly treasure. Caveman didn't have to worry about his house being ground into sticks. If his cave was flooded, he could just walk up a hill and set up housekeeping in another cave. Certainly, evolved mankind has managed to adapt to extremes of temperature and climate, but he will never conquer the weather.

No amount of planning or insurance or prayer can prevent Mother Nature from wreaking havoc when she decides to do so. About all we can do is cross our fingers and hope that natural disasters will continue their tendency to bypass us.

43

Cruising for Clothing

The details of our Castles along the Rhine and Danube cruise have been arranged. Frequent Flier miles will get us to the city of embarkation, and cancellation insurance will assure that our cruise fare won't be lost if there's an emergency. Post-cruise excursions and hotels have been reserved. What's left to do – besides lose a few pounds? Organize our wardrobes, of course.

Unlike vacations during which you stay in a hotel, a cruise means that you will be crossing paths with the same people three times a day for a week or longer. I don't know about you, but for that kind of exposure I need a *lot* of clothes. To be seen in the same outfit twice at dinner? I'd sooner show up in my underwear, although, come to think of it, a few designers have seen to it that some of our young sisters now appear to be wearing their slips and bras in public.

The summer clothes I've been wearing for my exciting life around here – visits to the Giant Eagle and Costco, are feeling pretty shopworn. Worn out is more like it. So I need to assemble a cruise wardrobe that might elicit compliments from my fellow cruisers. Ever the optimist, off I go in mid-June, in search of summer clothes.

Who am I kidding? One quick look around the display of garments has me wondering, where *are* the summer clothes? What do I find for sale in the middle of June? Long-sleeved jackets in autumnal earth tones – the clothing I will be buying (on sale) in November, when the clothes for next spring will have begun taking up the racks.

What is it with this jumping the seasons that retailers do to us? There was a feature on the *Today* show the other morning – frustrated souls like me, looking for summer clothes in July. Who ever heard of such a thing? A little girl practically in tears said, "I just wanted to buy a bathing suit." In July? Where has this child been? If she wanted a bathing suit, she should have bought it in April. July? Not this year, kiddo.

The sale racks contain the crammed-together dregs of summer merchandise, items that not even a self-respecting homeless person would want to be seen in. And finding acceptable white slacks is out of the question. There haven't been any of those around since mid-May. I spotted two pairs and tried them on. One came down so low in the front I would have needed a bikini wax to wear them. The other pair, although it fit in the hips, was so big around the middle that a grapefruit could have rested comfortably in the back of the waistband.

This dilemma occurs every year. And every year I think that things will be different next time around, that last year must have been an anomaly or my imagination. Surely, one can buy summer clothes in summer.

Discouraged and deflated after numerous fruitless searches, I hit upon the perfect solution: Catalogs! So I take a tour through the pages of a catalog from one of the many companies that send every week. Their daily appearance in my mailbox implores me, "Buy our clothes, PLEASE."

I order a hot-looking cranberry red spaghetti-strap top with matching pants and, along with it a smashing jacket, white with delicate black and red Oriental figures and plenty of room for my hips. Uh-oh! The jacket is on back order. That was two months ago. I'm still waiting for it.

Meanwhile, I find a suitable silk cover-up in the new fall merchandise at a store in the local mall. If the white jacket ever arrives, I will send it back immediately with a, "Sorry, you missed the boat" (literally!) note attached.

I express my frustration to the saleswoman who sells me the cover-up. She tells me, "I've been in retailing for thirty-two years, and it's always been this way."

Well it's time for it to stop being this way, and I believe that millions of women agree with me. Why people would purchase clothes for November when it's ninety-four degrees outside is a mystery. It only encourages the fashion-forward, first-out-of-the-gate marketers of the clothing we put on our backs. Because of them, I have been safeguarding my weary white slacks as well as most of my other hot weather garments for the cruise. My summer wardrobe has consisted of khaki and taupe.

According to Ken Perkins, president of the Research Firm Metrics LLC, "Strong sales in June left stores with very little inventory…and hot weather hurt sales of fall clothing." Well duh, Mr. Perkins. Haven't we had hot weather for the last several thousand summers?

Please – present us with something to buy in July that we can wear in July and we will buy it. Some of us don't get around to shopping for clothing for the season until the season has actually arrived. What a novel concept.

44

Sometimes It Takes a While

I brought a souvenir umbrella back from Paris decorated with the words "Paris" and "France" intermingled with tiny images of the Eiffel Tower. The Eiffel Tower is the undisputed symbol of Paris and of France and the most visited paid monument in the world. More than 250 million people have visited it since it was built 122 years ago.

Although I've been reading more novels than ever thanks to book clubs, radio and podcast reviews, and word of mouth, every once in a while I settle down with a non-fiction volume to learn something about the real world – the world of today or the world that used to be. I was recently told of a book about the building of the Eiffel Tower, which might sound a little dull. But take my word for it, this is one interesting book.

Its complete title – unwieldy for sure – is *Eiffel's Tower: And the World's Fair Where Buffalo Bill Beguiled Paris, the Artists Quarreled and Thomas Edison Became a Count*. The author is Jill Jonnes.

I've been to the Eiffel Tower a couple of times, but have never made it past ground level. It is an astonishing edifice not only because of its unique design but also because of its enormity. You cannot imagine how massive it is until you are standing in front of it.

Its construction was a feat of engineering, the likes of which had never been attempted. Upon its completion, it became the tallest structure in the world, at 984 feet, and remained so until the Chrysler Building in New York City was completed forty-one years later, in 1930.

I'll leave it to you to discover the amazing things Jill Jonnes reveals about Buffalo Bill, Annie Oakley, Thomas Edison, and scores of others, while I tell you about the Eiffel Tower.

Built for the Paris World's Fair of 1889, its designer, engineer Gustave Eiffel, already had an international reputation as a builder of bridges. But from the beginning, he was confronted by obstacles that would have caused an ordinary mortal to give up in disgust. There were frustrating delays, troubles with the workers, and punishing weather. He was embroiled in a prickly relationship with the Otis company, which would eventually, after months of acrimonious negotiations, be hired to install elevators in the tower. The French government had been resistant to allowing the work to be done by an American company, but they relented, acknowledging that the Otis designs were far superior to anything submitted by the French.

Eiffel had his detractors. Those from the highest echelons of the French art world did everything they could think of to berate the tower's design. All manner of campaigns were mounted and petitions circulated, signed by artists and writers – some of whose names you would recognize – disparaging the work, lamenting it as a "dizzily ridiculous tower dominating Paris like a black and gigantic factory chimney, crushing all beneath its barbarous mass," a "soulless vulgarity," and "a funnel planted on its fat butt." The most scurrilous accusation the critics tried to give traction was that Eiffel was a Jew. He was not.

The carping aesthetes had their say, but Eiffel had legions of influential supporters, and the public were enthralled by the tower and came to see it in record numbers. The makers of souvenirs began to cash in mightily as the tower was represented "with pen, pencil and brush," on handkerchiefs, in chocolate and marzipan, and in an avalanche of every imaginable kind of reproduction in all sizes and at all prices.

The contract for the Eiffel Tower specified that it was to be torn down after twenty years. Imagine – that wonder of creativity could have been cast into memory in 1909. Only when it was discovered how useful it was in radio communication, leading up to World War I, was it allowed to remain. And, as they say, the rest is history.

Revolutionary ideas can shock and frighten us. We think that the creator is a madman, that his ideas are bizarre, and that soon enough he will realize such and sink into obscurity. Think Picasso's cubism, Stravinsky's "Rite of Spring," or other classic works that were reviled when first presented to the masses.

Do you think that Andy Warhol's fellow students at Carnegie Mellon would have predicted, in 1949, that

he would become an internationally revered innovator
and be honored with a museum bearing his name, the
largest museum in America dedicated to a single artist?
I doubt it.

Some of you may want to hurl brickbats at me for
mentioning this person, and I may deserve it. But regardless of what you think of Lady Gaga, she is a phenomenon and a huge success. With her off-the-wall
outfits and outrageous hairstyles, she has a vision that we
don't yet understand. It will take the passage of several
decades before her impact can be assessed. Remember
Elvis? Remember the Beatles?

Sometimes it takes a while for the new to be accepted, for its value and legitimacy to be recognized.
Geniuses like Gustave Eiffel have vision and a determi-
nation that we ordinary mortals cannot fathom. And
they will not be deterred.

45

Money Matters, Lessons Learned

A few months ago, I noticed a mysterious charge on my VISA bill. It was always for $29.95 and under a variety of names such as Weight Counselor, MD; Fit Mentor, MD; and Diet Guru. Obviously weight control plan(s), but although I could have stood to lose a few pounds, I didn't recall ordering anything bearing those names.

I'll admit that I hadn't been carefully examining my monthly statements, so it took more than a year for me to realize that something was going on that wasn't kosher. I called the number on the statement and asked exactly what it was that I had been paying $29.95 a month for. I had received no merchandise or services that I could think of. I wasn't getting a satisfactory explanation but hammered away at the operator until she agreed to send me a three-month refund. I then tossed in a final sally that I would be calling the attorney general of Texas, where the charges originated. That was the last I heard of it. For a while. Then one day, several months later, there came in the mail a check for $359.40, the rest of the charges I had paid. That threat to call the attorney general evidently had the desired effect.

We all know by now that when we call to buy something advertised on the radio or "As Seen on TV," the operator tries to sell us additional merchandise. And sometimes we're signed up for things without realizing it and it's up to *us* to notice and put a stop to it. I'm lucky that this episode turned out the way it did, and it taught me, once and for all, to be sure I know what I'm agreeing to over the phone and, above all, not to assume that all of the charges on my credit card are legitimate. My statements will be microscopically scrutinized.

A couple of years ago, while traveling in Brazil, headed for the Amazon, I was puzzled that when I tried to use my VISA card and it was rejected. How come? I belong to an identity theft protection company called LifeLock whose ads you've probably heard on the radio. They really do keep an eye on your transactions and evidently, when charges from Brazil started coming in, my account was flagged. I had enclosed a note with my VISA payment telling them that we would be away and for how long, but I had neglected to notify LifeLock. I should have *called*, not written, to both companies and told them when we were leaving and where we would be.

Same thing happened in Hawaii last winter when Kmart charges from Kawai popped up. VISA called asking me to verify that we indeed were in Hawaii and that I had indeed been buying toothpaste and panty hose at a Kmart in Kawai.

Two days before leaving on a recent vacation outside of the U.S., on August 12, I discovered that my seldom-used Citizens Bank ATM card was missing. A check of recent statements showed that it had last been used at a nearby supermarket on June 13. However, when I called the store I was told that they indeed had found my card, but their policy is to destroy unclaimed cards after twenty-four hours. Woe is me. Don't they have my phone number in their vast computer system? Couldn't they have given me a buzz?

There I was, about to travel to several foreign countries, and no ATM card. And my husband, who is of the old, *really* old school, has never used an ATM card and was useless in this situation.

I had always been aware that credit cards can be used for quick cash but had never used mine for that purpose. So I set about examining all of the little slips of paper in my file cabinet, dating back to the Stone Age, which contained a PIN number. Finally, I came up with one that looked like the right one, went to Walgreen's ATM and – praise the Lord – it worked. Now all I had to do was *remember* the number. I jotted it down in a safe place and voila! – it worked in the ATM machines in the cities we visited. Lessons learned? Not to leave my ATM card in the machine, *and* keep track of my PIN numbers.

The day after we got home from our most recent trip I checked my VISA statement online and discovered a charge for $436 from our hotel in Belgium. As far as I knew we had spent only $60, for room service. I emailed them and got a reply within a few hours. (I'm transcribing it here exactly as the gentleman wrote it, because his English is charming. French and Dutch are spoken in Belgium):

"We thank you for your mail which we have well received...I have taken a look on the invoice and indeed upon check out we have taken the payment of 41euros for the incidentals. When I look on the 30th of August, when you have done your check in, we have asked you for a credit card to guarantee for the incidentals. This amount equals an authorization of 300 euros [$436] that we had blocked. But since it is a credit card, it is merely an authorization and not a charge. After check out this was released from our part and might take a couple of working days before your bank has processed it. If an issue would remain, please do not hesitate to contact us back."

Well I'll be hornswoggled. I had never heard of such a thing. I'm perfectly used to hotels asking for a credit card at check-in, but I had never had a "just in case" amount actually charged to my account as a matter of course. The cynic in me suspects that the hotel hopes that a few departed guests won't notice the charge and just pay it.

So – caveat emptor, buyer beware, or something to that effect. Merchants and financial institutions have figured out plenty of ways to get money from you. Examine your statements, keep track of your ATM card, be sure there's enough money in your account to cover unexpected charges, and make sure your credit card company (and in my case LifeLock) knows when you're leaving and each place you'll be visiting, especially if some of them are off the beaten track.

It's hard enough for us to hang on to our money without letting other people, who figure we're not paying attention, dig into our pockets and help themselves.

46

Gratitude

In her book, *Simple Abundance: A Daybook of Comfort and Joy,* author Sarah Ban Breathnach suggests writing down five things a day for which to be grateful or that bring us pleasure. Some of us spend so much time grumbling, focused on everything that's wrong in our lives, that there's not much space left for thinking about the many positives that we experience each day, which we take for granted.

Not until my mother spent her last days in a retirement home did I realize how wonderful it is simply to be able to come and go as one likes, to shop, to decide on meals, to have the capacity to be an autonomous human being. I keep that in mind when it's time to change the sheets, a chore that I detest. I think about the many who would love to be able, physically, to change the sheets on a bed or perform any of the other odious household chores that most of us would like to avoid.

I decided to make a list of my own, some of which you might find laughable. But it is my life, and I get to choose what little things, no matter how innocuous, lift my spirits. Making my list at the end of the day is useful because I get to re-experience those momentary pleasures such as:

- Accomplishing a long put-off task. Finally washing that expanding sack of panty hose.
- Trying a new recipe that turns out well and goes into the "For Company" file.
- Running into an old friend whom I'm genuinely happy to see.
- Finding, on sale, an item that is already on my shopping list.
- Getting a check in the mail along with the flyers and catalogs.

And as inconsequential as it might seem, not until I started making my little lists did I realize how important parking is in my life. There's not much that can happen in an ordinary day that makes me happier than finding a great parking space. And although I know that exercise is important, walking in particular, I climb down from my treadmill, drive to the mall, and search for the closest possible parking space even if it means driving around in circles for ten minutes.

Comedian and antique car buff Jay Leno recently joked about an event where a fancy, vintage car was being auctioned off. He said that it was so hard to find a place to park that the sponsors would have made more money by auctioning off a few parking spaces.

All of this shows that it doesn't really take much to make us happy. Many of us think that if we win the lottery we'll be happy. That's a fantasy that persists despite mountains of evidence to the contrary. Most lottery winners not only do not become instantly happy, often their lives fall apart, either because they have no idea how to handle a huge sum of money or because they eventually realize that their lack of personal satisfaction has nothing to do with their financial state.

Maybe the beginning of this new year is a good time to think of all the things for which we can be grateful and how it's the simple things, not sudden wealth, that give us a lift. It's too easy, dare I say too *normal,* to take the positives for granted.

At the top of my list page I've written, "All the usual stuff, plus..." The "usual stuff" would include the fact that I'm alive. Agatha Christie wrote: "I like living. I have sometimes been wildly, despairingly, acutely miserable, racked with sorrow, but through it all I still know quite certainly that just to *be* alive is a grand thing." So, if you're alive, you're on the winning team.

The "usual stuff" also includes good health, for however long it lasts; interesting, caring friends and family; a nice warm house to live in; plenty of nourishing food; and what I call "safe passage," that is, the good fortune to have navigated the highways and byways without running my car up a pole or backing over someone in the supermarket parking lot.

It's our gratitude for the simple things, stitched together, that helps us to view our lives as happy.

Self-help author and teacher Melody Beatty says, "Gratitude unlocks the fullness of life. It turns what we have into enough, and more. It turns denial into acceptance, chaos to order, confusion to clarity. It can turn a meal into a feast, a house into a home, a stranger into a friend. Gratitude makes sense of our past, brings peace for today, and creates a vision for tomorrow."

Starting today, I'm going to try harder to be aware of the simple abundance of good things that come my way and remember that just by being here I'm a winner in the lottery of life.

47

What Should We Know?

My husband and I enjoy watching the first half hour of the *Tonight Show*, especially the "Jaywalking" feature when Jay Leno asks people strolling around Los Angeles questions about current events, famous people, or whatever else might be fodder for a few laughs. I suspect the bit is popular not only because it's hilarious but also because it gives us viewers an opportunity to feel superior to the people chosen, whose answers reveal them to be clueless about the most ordinary facts, facts that you would expect everyone to know. Shown a photo of Hillary Clinton? Not a clue. A photo of Kim Kardashian? No problem. True, most of the respondents are young. They know popular culture, but they know little about the people who might actually make a difference in their lives.

Maybe the kids who spend all of their time playing video games have the right idea. Perhaps ignorance *is* bliss. Wouldn't you and I feel better if we had no idea what's been going on in Congress or with the European Union? People who have no interest in the stock market or who can't identify the president of Iran probably sleep a lot better than we do.

You have to wonder if you'd remember your own name if you were suddenly stopped by a celebrity, who thrusts a microphone at you and asks a question in front of a film crew and a crowd of gawking onlookers. It's possible you'd remember your name but you probably wouldn't remember who's buried in Grant's tomb. So maybe we shouldn't be so critical of Jay's "questionees."

Some of the funniest answers are those in which the respondents are asked to complete a maxim such as "A stitch in time..." They *never* know the last words of sayings that we learned in grade school. And although their answers occasionally make sense on a certain level, they are still wrong. "What's good for the goose is good for the *chicken*," might make some kind of sense although it's not the right answer, but it *is* funny. And after all, we don't know how many prospects were questioned who might have known that the answer is *gander*, but would never have been chosen for the show.

A contestant on *Who Wants to Be a Millionaire?* who said she had majored in English literature, was given a list of rhyming words such as *shore, implore, before, adore, etc.* She was asked to pick which, among the choice of four poetic works, is known for its many words that rhyme with those on the list. One of the choices was "The Raven," which most of us know opens with, "Once upon a midnight dreary..." and ends with "Quoth the raven, nevermore."

The contestant did not know the answer and jumped the question, saying she had skipped the poetry portion of English literature. Hunh?

Now I'm not much of a poetry buff, nor did I major in English literature, but I do know Edgar Allen Poe's "The Raven." Isn't it one of the poems we read in high school along with "Paul Revere's Ride"?

Sometimes when a contestant doesn't know an answer it's because the relevant event took place when they were in diapers. On a recent *Jeopardy!* one of the answers was, "This woman succeeded her late husband as a senator from Minnesota to become the state's first woman senator." The question? "Who was Muriel Humphrey?" The widow of the late senator and vice president Hubert Humphrey, Mrs. Humphrey went to the senate in 1978. For my husband and me it was a no-brainer. But none of the three young contestants knew the answer.

Because it has been so long since I was in school, I know little about what students are now required to learn. Do they study standard works of literature or have the classics been deemed irrelevant? Do today's high school graduates recognize, "It was the best of times, it was the worst of times," the opening phrases of Dickens' *A Tale of Two Cities*?

Educational criteria have changed, curricula have changed, standards have changed, and seldom in the direction we'd like. So perhaps we should be a little patient with people who don't know what we think they should know.

The young woman on *Millionaire* didn't do herself or our educational system a favor by not recognizing "The Raven." Maybe I'm overreacting, but I think she should be disappointed with those who allowed her to earn a degree with an incomplete education.

How many classes of unwitting students will assume she's qualified to guide them through English literature – poetry excluded?

48

What's With These Giant Handbags?

I'll probably offend half of my female readers by asking the following question: What in the world do so many women carry in those enormous handbags? I seem to be one of a minority who don't carry a bag big enough to lug around a bowling ball.

I've always been a shoulder bag girl figuring why not have two free hands for carrying things? But it isn't easy to find shoulder bags these days. Instead, the shelves are groaning under the weight of huge, two-handle bags, some of them weighted down with all manner of bling – gold and silver doodads, chains, studs, and other paraphernalia – that look like they could carry you through a weekend in the Amazon.

I find myself wondering several things such as what is *in* these bags that must be carried around all the time? How much of the contents is carried day in and day out when the chance it will be needed is remote, if not nonexistent? What is it that their owners need on a daily basis that I don't need?

My favorite daytime bag weighs nine ounces. It has a zipper compartment on the outside that holds my credit cards, driver's license, receipts, and cash. That means I don't have to worry about carrying or losing a wallet.

Inside are my comb, compact and lipstick, chewing gum, dental floss, cell phone, a pen, eyeglass and anti-bacterial wipes, a couple of Kleenex, and my car key fob. When I need an umbrella, a small one fits inside and my sunglasses case can be squeezed in. I usually carry the bag on my shoulder but for extra security I can pass the strap over my head and wear it across my body.

Of course I wouldn't use my little bag for travel, but I seldom carry my passport, boarding passes, magazines, toothbrush and lunch to the doctor's office or the Giant Eagle. Maybe I should consider buying a jumbo bag. That way, I could put my groceries right into it and avoid the "paper or plastic?" dilemma.

I recently conducted a little survey on Facebook. And plenty of women, on both sides of the handbag divide, were quick to state their preference. One tells me, "I bought a smaller, more compact bag last year. I was tired of searching through a large space for what I wanted, which had sunk to the bottom. Now everything is easily accessible. I carry a wallet, credit card case, coupon holder, small make-up bag, Kleenex and keys."

Another one, who is evidently a fan of Arbor Day, writes, "Mine is a Mary Poppins bag. I carry my Nook and lots of junk and unidentifiable things. Maybe a tree."

Yet another is such a big-bag enthusiast that I suspect you'd have to pry hers from her by holding her down with your knee. She declares, "I'm addicted to huge handbags. They are the greatest thing that has ever happened in fashion."

Whoa. That's really saying something.

She goes on, "My small bags were always overstuffed. I carry my camera, my wallet, a check book, three or four pens, tissues, Handi-Wipes, sun- and reading glasses, a small makeup bag, cell phone, keys, small scissors, a tiny flash light, a calendar, coupons for that day's shopping, a handbag hanger, and a tiny note pad. I have the organizer inserts that can quickly be lifted and shifted to the next color bag."

Mercy me. This lady is prepared for all emergencies. It's surprising that she's not carrying a stethoscope and blood pressure cuff in case she has to resuscitate someone at Target. And if she needed to carry a bottle of water or extra shoes, she might need a second bag!

Obviously, carrying around all of that stuff lowers her anxiety level. She doesn't have to worry about forgetting anything, because *everything* is already, um, in the bag. And, as she has numerous inserts for various categories of *stuff*, you might say that she's lugging around a bag of bags.

She concludes by adding, "The leather of some large handbags is heavy enough to be a bother, but, in the long run, it's all about a great looking bag!" Aha! – the truth comes out. She's among those who will risk shoulder and back injury to carry "a great looking bag!"

Which brings me to another point: It has never seemed to me that carrying these giant bags is good for the neck and shoulders. In fact, Dr. Oz says that one of the biggest reasons for common pain is heavy purses. "Your shoulder is kind of like a jigsaw puzzle. You have the upper arm bone, the clavicle or collarbone and the shoulder blade all meeting at the same point. But there is no socket that holds them in place. They just kind of float in air, which is why your shoulder is both the most mobile and unstable joint." And as a recent sufferer of rotator cuff difficulties, I would add, among the trickiest to repair.

So – should you be considering buying a mammoth satchel, you might take a minute to think about how Dr. Oz, and your shoulder, would feel about it.

49

Hitting the Wall

A few of my friends, a very few, do not do email. If I wish to communicate with them I must do so by phone, by snail mail, or carrier pigeon. They and my husband are the only people with whom I come in frequent contact who don't communicate via computer and who neither own nor wish to own one. This is difficult for those of us who reside in the computer universe to understand. I can't remember what life was like before I was taken captive by my computer. Ordinarily, when I want my husband to see something that arrives via computer, I print it out. But I occasionally summon him to my office to view something that requires way too much ink to print, such as political bumper stickers or funny cat pictures.

Leaving him on his own to scroll down the screen is futile. He is left-handed, and if you can imagine how an experienced computer user would fare if suddenly called upon to operate a mouse with his left hand, you can understand how out of sync my husband feels. When I go back to check on him, he's on a completely different page or the screen has gone blank. "What did you *do*?" I ask. "I don't *know*," he replies.

My first computer arrived in 1995, and I haven't been the same since. I would probably have learned all thirty-two Beethoven sonatas and written a few best-sellers by now if I hadn't spent so many hours of the last seventeen years surfing the Internet and writing email. To be able to communicate with friends near and far or come up with the most arcane bits of information within seconds is a dream come true, and I've taken full advantage.

But the recent wave of social media suggests that email is a twentieth century phenomenon. In the twenty-first century, Facebook and Twitter and texting have become the currency of communication, and if you don't spend a few hours a day checking your notifications, you can forget learning about what's happening with most of your friends.

Although I realize that social media are changing the world in important ways – such as helping regimes to topple – the notion of going onto Twitter and sharing my every thought with the world is an unpleasant prospect. It is disconcerting, when I click on the Merriam Webster link to look up a word and see, at the bottom of the page, my Facebook face beside a little box that wants me to type in *why* I was looking up the word. It's not the entire world's business why I was looking up *gastro-jejunostomy* or *heuristics*. When it's necessary for them to have that information I'll make sure they do.

It used to be that when a new technology came along we were given several years to enjoy it before it became obsolete. Remember tape recorders? How wonderful it was to be able to record our own voices or instruments right in our living rooms, where shelves were laden with boxes of five and seven-inch reels. We enjoyed that technology for nearly fifteen years until cassettes came along sending the cumbersome reel-to-reel tapes to the attic.

The Victor company made it to the front page of *The New York Times* when, in 1925, it introduced the groundbreaking Victor Orthophonic Victrola, described as "an acoustical record player specifically designed to play electrically recorded discs." That was the beginning of the 78 rpm revolution that lasted until long-playing 33's came along, in the late forties, freeing us from the heavy, breakable discs that had to be turned over or changed every few minutes. LP's became the playback media of choice until the compact disc arrived in the early '80s. CDs have been the media of choice ever since, at least up until now.

In a recent issue of *Automotive News*, it was disheartening to read, "CD players, beloved by baby boomers, head for the exit." It says that auto makers want to get rid of optical drives – that is CD and DVD players – because they're expensive and appeal mainly to older motorists. So, Grandpa, your beloved CD's are being readied for the trash heap.

I've always considered myself up to date, but I'm beginning to feel as if I'm being dragged along by a technology train that's going too fast. Syndicated tech expert Leo Laporte, speaking about our being trapped into two-year cell phone contracts, says, "That's going to have to change because technology is moving so fast that nobody wants to keep a cell phone for two years anymore." Built-in obsolescence has become immediate obsolescence. Less than two years after the original iPad was introduced, the iPad *3* is set to come out any minute. Is my iPad 1 already an antique? In today's world, absolutely.

So for now, I'd like a little more time to savor the hi-tech marvels that surround me at the moment before going on to the next wave of miracles. You can tweet and text to your heart's content. But for the time being, I've hit the wall.

50

New Food

A couple of years ago, while channel surfing from my treadmill, I happened upon a chef-type individual who was applying a device – which turned out to be a blow torch – to a substance that turned out to be food. That was my introduction to a style, or perhaps I should call it a philosophy of food preparation called molecular gastronomy by some, although the practitioners of this avant garde approach to cooking dislike that name, preferring to call it "modernist."

I soon learned that this revolution was begun by a fellow near Barcelona named Ferran Adrià, who is considered by many to be the best chef in the world. And his restaurant, El Bulli (boo-YEE, or bully if you prefer), earned him three Michelin stars before it closed in 2011 to be reopened in 2014 as a creativity center, a kind of think-tank for creative cuisine and gastronomy.

From Wikipedia I learned: "In the late 1980s, Adrià began performing cooking experiments that would forever change culinary history. His lab-like experiments apply science to culinary practices and cooking phenomena. His creations are designed to surprise and enchant his guests, but the importance of flavor is always the ultimate goal.

"Adrià is perhaps best known for creating *culinary foam,* now used by chefs all over the world, which consists of natural flavors (sweet or savory) mixed with a natural gelling agent. The mixture is placed in a whipped cream canister from which the foam is forced out with the help of nitrous oxide."

Another technique favored by the modernist chef, called *sous vide,* under vacuum, is a method of cooking food sealed in airtight plastic bags in a water bath for a long period – seventy-two hours is not unusual – at an accurately determined temperature much lower than normally used for cooking, typically around 140 degrees Fahrenheit. The intention is to cook the item evenly, not overcook the outside, while still keeping the inside at the same 'doneness' and the food juicier.

By now you're probably wondering why I'm telling you all of this. First of all, I mentioned molecular gastronomy to a friend recently, and she looked at me quite blankly. She had never heard of this new cuisine, which I found interesting because I think of her as someone who is up on new things. So I assume she isn't alone in being unfamiliar with this culinary revolution.

For the past couple of years there has been a restaurant in Oakmont, a Pittsburgh suburb, called *notion, where* cuisine in the molecular gastronomy style is featured. My husband and I had a chance to try it before it closed recently to relocate within the city and, although its creation was a much-publicized labor of love for well known chef David Racicot, we were not altogether enchanted by the experience. And let me emphasize that we're willing to attribute our reaction to our lack of sophistication and not to this star chef's culinary skills.

To reinforce the fact that this would not be an ordinary meal, our menus were delivered in black manila envelopes. (My husband asked the waiter if they had been kept secure by Price-Waterhouse.) The printed sheet inside listed four starters, four entrees, two desserts, and the chefs tasting menu (no apostrophe included).

It took a few minutes for us to realize that the microscopic superscript numbers following the dishes were the prices, e.g., white beans^{12}, pork^{28}. The chefs tasting menu, which had to be ordered by everyone at the table, was a somewhat daunting "seven courses^{85}/paired with wine^{115}" per person. The minuscule representation of the prices made me suspect that if they could have kept the prices a secret they would have.

Before our main courses were served, we were each presented with a small, complimentary glass of lemon foam. It was up to us whether to drink it or spoon it. What there was of it had an intensely lemony zing that woke up our taste buds.

There were four of us, so we each ordered a different starter and a different entrée. My starter was cauliflower: "several forms, red curry, cider." When it arrived it was esthetically interesting but not recognizable as cauliflower. I can't recall now to what processes the cauliflower had been subjected, although the waiter had probably explained it, at considerable length, as he did everything on the menu.

My husband ordered the risotto: "shrimp, saffron, citrus, zucchini." I assume it was all there, but what piqued our curiosity were the stiff black sheets of something balanced on top of the dish. We couldn't imagine what they were and it wasn't mentioned in the menu. Had the waiter told us that the risotto would be topped with Parmesan crisps colored with squid ink? If so, we had missed that part, and the presentation was startling to behold.

Our meats and fishes were prepared *sous vide*. And although the textures were pleasant, because of the low temperature at which they were cooked, they were barely warm.

We attempted to sample some of our companions' dishes, but it was awkward to pass food around to three other diners, plus, by the time all three had tasted your dish, there wasn't much left for you to taste. This is not a place where dieters need fear overeating or from which one takes home a doggie bag.

All of the dishes, if that's not too mundane a description, were lovely to behold and for the most part pleasing, but not spectacularly so. Nothing about the experience prompted me to rush to my calendar to pencil in the next visit.

My husband and I discussed the meal for the next several days. We agreed that it was an interesting experience, which served up plenty of fodder for conversation. But in the long run we decided we would rather that such a pricey meal be a little more delicious and a little less interesting.

51

In the Ear *of the Beholder*

They say that that beauty is in the eye of the beholder. We might say something similar about music – that it is in the *ear* of the beholder.

In a spirited discussion with a friend recently, she put forth the opinion that heavy metal music is *crap*. Aside from the fact that *crap* might not be the best choice of word to use in polite discourse, I found myself unaccountably disputing her assessment nearly to the point of defending heavy metal music. I was put off by the "end of discussion" nature of her pronouncement. And instead of listening to my better angels and responding with an affirmative, "You're *right*," I countered with, "It's crap to *you*."

This lady is an occasional participant in Gilbert and Sullivan opera productions, and I finally became so undone by her vehemence that I shot back, "Well some people think that Gilbert and Sullivan is crap." And she couldn't give me much of an argument.

That very night I dreamt that I was playing the beginning phrases of Rachmaninoff's Piano Concerto No. 3, the one that was featured in the movie *Shine*. I woke up with it still swirling in my mind and thinking, "What music could evoke any more blissful a feeling than the simple, single-line melody that begins the piece?" Well, to the ears of many, plenty. I doubt if Jay Z or the Foo Fighters get especially worked up by Rachmaninoff. Then again, maybe they do. Who knows what musical variety they enjoy when they're out of the spotlight?

There is nothing more personal than one's taste in music and one's reaction to it. Music moves me to dance and conduct, much to the consternation of my husband who would prefer that these eruptions not take control of me, as they often do, when I'm driving.

I observe the staid audiences at classical music concerts and wonder how they are able to sit still – nary a head bob nor a foot tap – unlike the audiences at rock concerts who feel free to wave and sway in response to the music.

Lest you think that classical music is the only music that gets my juices flowing, the wall to wall coverage of the death of Whitney Houston reminded me of what an incredible legacy of beautiful singing she left behind. "I Will Always Love You" became her anthem, in life and in death. But there were so many others, just as beautiful if not as well known. The refrain of one, "Where do broken hearts go, can they find their way home, back to the open arms of a love that's waiting there?" is a heartbreaking expression of loss. Yet, when I take my video player to my husband at the breakfast table, my eyes brimming with tears, he, sweet guy that he is, barely looks up from his morning paper. I want him to experience the music the way I do, but that will never happen.

He's moved by Mahler and Delius and Elgar. It's all in the ear of the beholder.

We experience music on a visceral level, from the inside out. It allows us to express or experience our deepest emotions in acceptable ways, and no one can predict which music might fill that need in our lives. Perhaps this manner of human expression is why all music except religious chants is banned by the Taliban. They are aware of the power of music to free our emotions and consider emotions unacceptable except in the service of their god.

Where we are listening to music affects our reactions as much as the music itself. I jokingly say that I can tolerate nearly any kind of music except mariachi. Yet, in the right context – visiting Mexico, as I did recently, or dining in a Mexican restaurant – it would seem strange to hear anything else. The music colors the experience, and vice versa. The same could be said of Spanish Flamenco, New Orleans jazz, Swiss yodeling or Japanese samisen.

Music evokes feelings of time and place. Think of a French accordion playing "La vie en rose" or "Irma la Douce." We are immediately transported to a sidewalk cafe on the Champs-Élysées or a dimly-lit bistro on the Boulevard St. Germain.

And remember the songs you danced to when you were in high school or dating? When you hear them you are transported back in time. "They're playing our song!"

American popular music has taken over the world. No matter what other kinds of music young tastemakers are listening to in other countries, they know our pop stars. And when they listen, in concert or on recordings, they can imagine themselves looking cool on the streets of New York or L. A.

Me, I'd rather be on the Champs-Élysées. And there's nothing that can conjure that feeling better than the shimmery melodies of the French accordion.

Maybe you don't agree. But that's the way I hear it.

52

Culinary Crises

There seems to be an increasing number of people, especially young people, who don't know how to cook. I'm inclined to think it's more a matter of their not wanting to be bothered rather than not knowing how. If you can read, you should be able to cook *something*. Recipes abound, and many of them are simple enough to put together in case going out for every meal gets to be a drag or there doesn't happen to be a purveyor of prepared food around.

I learned to make Spanish rice at the age of ten, and since then, most of what has come out of my kitchen has been pretty good. But every once in a while my ability to put a decent meal on the table – aided by a dollop of common sense – fails me.

The other day I prepared a dinner that was supposed to be special, special because the protein component was sea scallops, which, considering what they cost, should be encrusted with emeralds. The recipe calls for scallops to be combined with mushrooms, garlic and shallots, and baked for ten minutes. The accompaniments were mock mashed potatoes, made with cauliflower, and a favorite of my husband's, lima beans, which I seldom serve because they're one of those starchy veggies that ratchet up the carb intake.

But despite my good intentions, the meal was a bust. The mushrooms were underdone, as were the lima beans. The cauliflower/potatoes had the proper texture and flavor, but they were lukewarm. It took longer than I expected for them to get hot in the microwave when they had been prepared ahead of time and reheated directly from the refrigerator.

I've been keeping house and cooking for more than forty years, and you would think I'd know how to cook a lima bean by now. And as many times as I've sautéed mushrooms, you might assume that I'd *know* when they had, as the recipe says, "given up their liquid." I thought they had surrendered their juices in this case, and figured that since the mixture was headed for a 450-degree oven, any additional cooking would be accomplished there. But that was not the case, and the mushrooms came out leathery, not a desirable quality in a mushroom.

The problem with the lima beans was that I simply didn't put enough water in the container to cook them sufficiently. A few of them exploded in the microwave. And the ones that remained intact, not stuck to the sides and ceiling of the microwave, required more effort to chew than a lima bean should.

Although my sweet husband *never* complains, the meal was such a disappointment that I launched into a litany of, "I'm-sorry-I'm-so-sorry," as if I were reciting the Rosary.

Unfortunately, most of us can recount a tale of a meal served to company that didn't go well. My most embarrassing culinary blunder happened when I invited eight people for a dinner that included the *Silver Palate's* Cornish Hens with Autumn Fruits, a variation on their famous Chicken Marbella, a recipe that created a stir in the late 70s because the marinade contained an entire head of garlic along with prunes and green olives. Back then we had never heard of anything quite so exotic.

I marinated the little birds in the robust concoction, placed them neatly in my turkey-roasting pan, poured the lovely marinade over them, and into the oven they went. But when the time came to serve them, oops – they weren't done. It hadn't occurred to me that the roasting pan, although it held the tiny fowls, wasn't big enough to allow the hot air to circulate properly. Thank heaven I owned a microwave by then so that the guests could enjoy another glass of wine while each individual hen was "finished" in the microwave.

Our next door neighbors hadn't been long moved in when I invited them to share two pheasants that a friend's husband had brought home, and which had been in our freezer for a while. I asked them if they liked pheasant and if they'd like to come for a pheasant dinner. Of course they said they would. What else could they say? For all I knew they were vegetarians.

So invite them I did and proceeded to serve the worst meal I've ever served anyone. They say that you shouldn't serve company dishes that you haven't first tried out on yourself. I couldn't do a trial run on pheasants. And throwing caution to the wind I decided to serve, along with the pheasants, a peculiar dish made of sautéed leeks, recommended as something that would go well with pheasant. I had never cooked leeks and didn't even know if I liked them. They tasted fine, but they were an odd addition to the meal, and the recipe made enough to feed the entire neighborhood.

Pheasant has a reputation of being *dry*. Research online and in cookbooks suggests that topping the birds with slices of the Italian bacon pancetta will keep them moist. Well maybe in some other universe they do, but those pheasants were the driest, chewiest substance I had ever attempted to eat. Part of the problem was that I couldn't figure out how long to leave them in the oven, so they ended up with the texture of pheasant jerky, if you can imagine such a thing.

And as if I hadn't already dug myself into a hole, I decided to try making crème brûlée for dessert. I bought cute little ramekins and a small torch and thought, "How hard can it be?" Well, evidently harder than I thought, because I couldn't get those little suckers to behave, couldn't get them to set, and absolutely couldn't get a crispy crust on top.

We got through the meal, the neighbors were gracious, and in the intervening years they have enjoyed a few good meals at our table.

Rachel Ray and the Food Network notwithstanding, most household cooks are not immune from making terrible blunders in the kitchen. There's an abundance of culinary booby traps waiting to snare us and bring us down with a thud. Unlike trained chefs, we thrash about searching for recipes that sound good, hoping that our efforts will be enjoyed by our family and friends and worthy of our time, effort and, above all, optimism.

53

They Call It a Restroom?

There are a lot of things you might get in there, but rest isn't one of them. Relief maybe, but not rest.

If you wanted to do yourself in, I can't think of a better way than by trying to extract toilet tissue from one of those enormous dispensers in public restroom stalls, where plunging your hand inside trying to find the end of the tissue often leads to contact with a serrated blade with which you might be able to slash your wrist if you're having a bad day.

Scientists have gotten us to the moon and back but they haven't yet figured out a way for us to extract a proper length of toilet tissue without anxiety, either because there are a few minutes when you fear that you will *never* find the end of the tissue, that if you manage to do so it will tear at the first little tug, or that there's a line of ladies anxiously waiting to use the facilities before the concert or play begins. Those industrial-size dispensers were designed to make *lots* of tissue available to *lots* of people in public places. But none of them works very well. So one often feels like tearing out one's hair while trying to tear out the tissue.

Years of experience has taught me always to measure out my tissue before performing my intended function because I don't want to be sitting or, worse yet, hovering, while trying to wrest the stuff from a balky dispenser. I know there's tissue in there. The question is, "Where the heck *is* it?" When I finally do get a grip on it, it is often so flimsy that I know I'd better pull gently or I'll have to start all over again.

I had an experience a few years ago at a local university that I will never forget. I'll spare you the details except to say that I was accompanying an important rehearsal; there was a roomful of singers and a conductor waiting for me to come back from a break.

Part of the dilemma was caused by the fact that the tissue was breaking and *shredding* to such an extent that I ended up waddling from stall to stall in a state of semi-dishabille – thank God there was no one else in there – trying to find a dispenser from which I might be able to pull down the needed amount. I wasn't very successful and went back to the rehearsal in a less pristine condition than I might have hoped. One would think that an institution that charges a middle class salary for a single year's tuition might be able to provide something other than the wispiest tissue available.

In a recent *Pittsburgh Post-Gazette* "Homemaking" column, Peter McKay addressed the assorted frustrations created by electronic sensors in public restrooms, and the fact that you're never quite sure if the sensor is going to sense, too soon or too late, that you have completed your mission. While his anxious moments occur inside the stall, mine happen mostly when I'm trying to brush my teeth at a sink, usually at an airport, where sensors are ubiquitous. Brushing one's teeth at an electronic faucet requires the reflexes of a Whack-a-Mole champ. Since the faucets are timed, you first have to wait for the sensor to decide it wants to emit a feeble spray, usually of warm water, so that you can moisten the brush that's holding the toothpaste.

Then, brushing done, the next trick is cupping enough water in your hand to rinse your mouth while other travelers, most of whom would never think of brushing their teeth in a public restroom, are wandering in and out casting, you fear, strange looks in your direction.

The next challenge is the towel dispenser. How, exactly, does one get the towels out? It used to be you could just pull down the edge of a towel and that was that. But now we're confronted by dispensers that have spooky red lights that know you are there, emit a little whiney hum, and extrude a towel. Others have levers, handles, and cranks. And there are barrel-shaped ones from which a length of towel can be yanked from the bottom if the last user left enough of a tail for you to get a grip on.

Regardless of the type of towel dispenser, any model is preferable to the old-fashioned hand dryer, which first appeared in 1948 and has been annoying us ever since. There's nothing like a visit to a restroom that provides no towels at all, just dryers, to ruin my day. I would much rather skulk back into a stall like the Pink Panther, grab a handful of tissue, and do the job myself than passively stand there looking around the room whistling Dixie, until my allotment of hot air is used up.

And speaking of stalls, I hope I won't be thrown into the pokey for confessing that whenever possible I use the handicap stall. It's not like using a handicap parking space. I mean, how long do I plan to stay in there? In the many years since handicap stalls first appeared, not once have I exited one and found a handicapped person waiting for me to emerge. In my opinion, *all* restroom stalls should open *out* so that you don't have to drag your clothing and belongings across the iffy toilet seat. It just ain't civilized.

There is one bright spot in the otherwise dispiriting world of restrooms, a new generation of hand dryer so powerful that you feel as if your hands might be ripped off at the wrist. If you haven't yet experienced the Dyson Airblade you're in for a whole new hand-drying experience. Like Dyson vacuum cleaners, they are super powerful and super expensive, in the $1200 range. So not too many public places are forking out those big bucks even though the dryers save a fortune in paper towels and cleanup. But honestly, I wouldn't mind paying a small fee to be turbo-dried by a Dyson.

And before I hop down from my soapbox – a word about soap. Actual soap, the liquid kind, seems to be disappearing. We now get to pump little gobs of foam into our hands. It feels as if we're washing our hands with air. But the label on the dispenser assures me that it's antibacterial air.

I realize that the establishments whose restrooms cause us to grit our teeth are really trying to give us a satisfactory experience while attempting to keep their costs down. The trouble is, their efforts aren't working very well. In an ideal world all towels would be terry cloth, like those in some cruise ships and private clubs. All users would neatly place their towel into the appropriate receptacle, turn the water off when they've finished, and not waste the soap. But this is not an ideal world, and until it is, we'll have to put up with these minor annoyances keeping in mind that there are still a lot of people in this world who have to get up in the middle of the night to use the facilities – outside.

54

Comic Relief

I read a lot of books, and many of them, although they're about topics I wish to know more about, are pretty grim – Hitler in the 20s, the horror of life in North Korea, the plight of blacks escaping the Deep South before the Civil Rights era, that of young Hungarian Jewish expatriates in Paris just before World War II, and early-onset Alzheimer's.

A constant diet of such dismal topics would surely put me into a funk were it not for the funny books that I sneak in among the gloomy ones. They say that humor is the best medicine, and I don't think anyone can deny the therapeutic effect of a good laugh.

If you happen to be looking for something to lift your spirits while relaxing on your patio, waiting in an airport lounge, or lying on the beach, here are a few suggestions.

Although I seldom read a book twice, I couldn't re-sist re-reading David Sedaris's *Me Talk Pretty One Day.* Sedaris, who comes from a family of funny people – his sister Amy has a few funny books of her own – is nearly always good for laughs. *Me Talk Pretty One Day* won me over from page one, when David is taken from class to "an unmarked door near the principal's office" by an "agent," who turns out to be a speech therapist.

Besides *Me Talk Pretty One Day,* whose title alludes to Sedaris's struggle to learn French when he finds out that he and his partner are going to be living in France, you might take a look at *Naked* or *Holidays on Ice.* And if you're a fan of audio books, track down a CD of "David Sedaris Live at Carnegie Hall." If that doesn't tickle your funny bone, you're in need of more than suggestions from me.

If you haven't read the prolific Bill Bryson you're in for a treat, as long as you pick your titles carefully. Although he has written many books about travel – in the U.S., England, and Australia – his more recent volumes have leaned toward serious topics, among them *A Brief History of Nearly Everything; Shakespeare: The World As Stage,* and, most recently, *At Home: A Short History of Private Life,* all of which are interesting but *not meant* to be funny.

However, *Neither Here nor There: Travels in Europe* and his other travel books are highly amusing, whether you're a traveler or not. If you're interested in learning about Australia pick up a copy of *In a Sunburned Country.* Or if you'd rather keep it on this side of the Atlantic, you can't go wrong with *I'm a Stranger Here Myself: Notes on Returning to America After 20 Years Away; The Lost Continent: Travels in Small-Town America;* or *A Walk in the Woods: Rediscovering America on the Appalachian Trail.*

Bryson's memoir *The Life and Times of the Thunderbolt Kid* caused one Amazon reader to be banished from his bedroom for laughing so loudly: "My wife trudged out of bed to decree that, if I insisted on continuing to read, I'd have to take it downstairs."

Although you might be unaware or only vaguely aware of comedienne Chelsea Handler – her fan base consists of females between eighteen and thirty-four – she is one of the hottest and wealthiest female entertainers in the business, described in *Time* magazine as "the most powerful one-woman media brand this side of Oprah or maybe Rachael Ray," and she is No. 33 on *Forbes Magazine's* list of the world's most powerful women. Who knew?

Are You There, Vodka? It's Me, Chelsea is undoubtedly funny, although it's not for the prudish. Handler's booze-forward, let-it-all-hang-out style won't be everyone's cup of tea, but if you're game, she'll provide you with a bucket of laughs.

Girl Walks into a Bar: Comedy Calamities, Dating Disasters, and a Midlife Miracle is a memoir by Rachel Dratch. Who is Rachel Dratch? She's the short and busty, slightly bug-eyed comedienne who was a featured performer on *Saturday Night Live* for seven years. When she left SNL she believed two things: that she was going to become the character Jenna on "30 Rock" and that she would never have children. Exactly the opposite occurred. Jane Krakowski got the role of Jenna, and, at age forty-four, Rachel gave birth to sweet little baby Eli, who barely escaped being named Hercules. Really. Dratch's candor and comic instincts make *Girl Walks into a Bar* both funny and touching.

While browsing Amazon's home page, I stumbled upon *You're Not Doing It Right: Tales of Marriage, Sex,*

Death, and Other Humiliations by Michael Ian Black. I wouldn't have expected to be so entertained by a guy young enough to be my grandson, but I found his tales hilarious in part because he is so truthful about himself and his feelings. His descriptions of new fatherhood ("I Hate My Baby") and buying a BMW ("I Am a Demographic") are worth the price of the book.

Although it might not crack you up, Augusten Burroughs' *Running with Scissors: A Memoir* is bound to entertain you, whether you find it amusing and appalling, or simply appalling. Described as "a funny, harrowing account of an ordinary boy's survival under the most extraordinary circumstances," I would have found it utterly implausible were it not for the fact that it is indeed a memoir, not fiction. Burroughs, whose mother and sisters are all, as Othello might have put it, "passing strange" – which is to say stranger than strange – is sent at the age of twelve to live at the home of his mother's psychiatrist who is even stranger.

What I find funny might leave you scratching your head. Humor is nothing if not personal. I will *never get* The Three Stooges, and I know I'm not alone. But I realize that millions find them the last word in funniness. But there are stories, jokes and situations that most of us can agree are funny. I've done my best to point you in the direction of a few things that tickled my funny bone hoping they might tickle yours and bring you relief, comic relief, from, among other things, the unfunny realities of the evening news.

In case you're curious, here is a list of the unfunny books I alluded to in Paragraph 1:

Hitlerland – Andrew Nagorski
Nothing to Envy – Barbara Demick
The Warmth of Other Suns – Isabel Wilkerson
The Invisible Bridge – Julie Orringer
Still Alice – Lisa Genova

55

More About Dining

On a recent tour of the Canadian Maritime provinces – Nova Scotia, New Brunswick and Prince Edward Island – I was discouraged, in one of our hotel dining rooms, from ordering the Pavlova, a fussy dessert of meringue topped with fruit and whipped cream. Evidently the meringue was collapsing that day. Meringue is notoriously temperamental and must have been affected by the moisture in the air from a day-long drizzle.

I didn't want to order the crème brûlée that my husband had ordered, and although I love chocolate and would love to have tried the yummy concoction on the menu, chocolate tends to keep me awake and give me heartburn. Options dwindling, the waiter suggested that I try the peppered strawberries on vanilla ice cream. I was dubious but agreed.

If nothing else, I learned that evening that I do not much care for peppered strawberries despite the waiter's assurances that "it's very popular." And it must be. It turned up on other menus, and there are many recipes online that involve peppered strawberries. Call me unadventurous, but I'll pass.

So many weird things are happening in the culinary world that it's a little hard to keep up with the young

237

tastemakers who, understandably, are not content to let our taste buds become jaded. But I'm not yet ready for ice cream like some of those pictured in a recent issue of *Time* – Black Chocolate Orange Sichuan Peppercorn or Goat Cheese with Marionberry Habanero Jam. Just reading about them gives me a hankerin' for Neapolitan.

And although I love bacon, I am not about to try Burger King's new bacon sundae. I subscribe to the old saying, "A place for everything and everything in its place." And a sundae, in my opinion, is not the place for bacon.

———

Included in my summer reading was *Yes, Chef,* a fascinating memoir by the much-heralded culinary star Marcus Samuelsson. If his name doesn't ring a bell, you've probably seen his striking countenance in magazines or on the Food Network. When I walked into the kitchenware department of Macy's a few days ago I quickly spotted his photo on a poster recommending the Calphalon collection of cookware.

Born in Ethiopia and raised in Sweden by adoptive parents, Samuelsson eventually made the United States his home. A person of prodigious talent and remarkable resolve, Samuelsson has become one of the world's most decorated chefs and has won every important culinary award beginning at age twenty-four with a three-star review from *The New York Times* for his flagship Manhattan restaurant Aquavit. And he was chosen to create the menu for the Obama's first state dinner hosting Prime Minister Manmohan Singh of India and his wife.

As he rose in the culinary world Samuelsson became obsessed with finding new tastes and combining non-traditional lists of ingredients. Reading about the dishes he creates, I understand more than ever that I know next to nothing about cooking. What I do in the kitchen compared with what Samuelsson and chefs at his level do is like the difference between *playing* "Chopsticks" and *composing* "Clair de lune." With his vast knowledge and sophisticated palate, he has created new flavor combinations, some of which have become his signature dishes. If you're curious about his very first signature dish, foie gras ganache – if you disapprove his use of foie gras, write to him, not to me – you can find the recipe online. The list of ingredients doesn't make my taste buds tingle, but I'm willing to be convinced should the occasion ever arise. Samuelsson says, "I've served my ganache to kings and starlets and three-star chefs and people who simply love food, and everywhere I go, the dish is a hit."

———

Having recently experienced some puzzling gastric symptoms, it was suggested that I might be gluten-intolerant. I have since learned that that is not the case, but I've become much more aware of the gluten-sensitivity issue. In our Canadian tour group there were two women who suffer from gluten intolerance, which, at worst, causes celiac disease, an autoimmune condition that attacks the small intestines and interferes with the absorption of important nutrients. The foods containing gluten are primarily wheat, barley, and rye.

One of the women was diagnosed thirty-two years ago. Her weight had fallen to eighty-seven pounds and a diagnosis was a long time coming. Back then hardly anyone had ever heard of celiac disease (also called sprue), and you certainly couldn't go into a supermarket and buy gluten-free *anything*. Now, there are gluten-free foods all over the place. Trader Joe's has a six-page list of items that are naturally gluten-free or specifically manufactured to be gluten-free.

Although the percentage of gluten-sensitive individuals is higher than I realized, it is still relatively small, although many I mention it to are either gluten sensitive or know someone who is. If you've experienced strange undiagnosed symptoms it wouldn't hurt to get yourself checked for gluten sensitivity. There is a blood test, but a biopsy is more conclusive.

In addition to vegetarian items, some restaurants are beginning to offer gluten-free choices. In fact Marcus Samuelsson mentions gluten-free cuisine in *Yes, Chef* saying that until recently chefs were unsympathetic to diners with special needs considering them finicky or unsophisticated. But they have become more accommodating, offering not only vegetarian choices, but also appetizing gluten-free dishes.

56

The Not–So- Friendly Skies

There are still some good things about flying – in an airplane, that is – but not many.

Arriving on time without crashing tops the list. Being spared the spectacle of some crazed individual – an ordinary citizen, or nowadays a member of the flight crew – freaking out, comes in at number two.

And although screaming infants and fussy toddlers do not pose a safety threat, the absence of such an annoyance is something for which to be grateful. Perhaps you recently read about a couple who brought along little bags of treats to give fellow passengers as a peace offering if or when their small children caused a ruckus. A nice gesture, but small comfort on a cross-country overnighter.

Although security screenings are supposed to make us feel safe, consider this: In mid-October a passenger dressed in a bullet-proof vest and flame-retardant pants was arrested at the Los Angeles airport after a number of items – get this – a smoke grenade, a gas mask, leg irons, body bags, a hatchet, billy clubs, a collapsible baton, duct tape, and a biohazard suit were found in his checked luggage. He was coming from Japan via South Korea where he evidently breezed through security. The

241

only thing he was charged with when he arrived in the United States was one count of transporting hazardous materials. Makes me wonder about my nail clippers and rat-tail comb being confiscated at the Manaus (Brazil) airport because security is so *strict* for planes coming to the U.S.

Compared to the way it used to be, flying has become a demoralizing affair. I'm not referring to the high heels and white gloves era, the *Mad Men* days. I'm talking about a mere fifteen or twenty years ago, before 9/11, and before the world became populated by so many who have lost their inhibitions and any sense of consideration for their fellow humans.

Declining revenues and escalating fuel prices have pretty much deflated what used to be a much anticipated experience. Where airlines used to coddle their customers to assure repeat business, they know we're going to fly no matter how badly we're treated, so they hold us upside down by our ankles and shake every bit of loose change from our pockets until our extremities go numb. As it is, we're already going numb from ever-shrinking leg room.

And in case emptying our pockets and packing us in like sardines weren't enough, we can lately count on the news to bring us a weird airline story at least once a week. Recently the seats on several American Airlines 757's decided to break loose from their moorings, pitching the passengers backwards onto those behind them like the occupants of the Red Chair on the Graham Norton Show*. Was it sabotage by striking employees? Nobody seems to know for sure although there's plenty of speculation. Whatever the cause, hundreds of planes were grounded for inspection causing hundreds of flights to be canceled. This during the week that *Newsweek* featured an article, "The Worst Job in America," about American Airlines president Tom Horton's struggle to the keep the airline afloat. I feel Mr. Horton's pain, but I'd think twice at this point about flying American. If the seats are coming loose what might come loose next?

We used to think of pilots as paragons of good behavior– skilled, strong, and steady. And flight attendants were courteous and efficient. We felt safe in their hands. But a recent spate of bad flight crew behavior has me wondering what's up. The first incident occurred a couple of years ago when JetBlue flight attendant Steven Slater engaged in a heated exchange with a passenger, said he was fed up, grabbed a couple of beers, and took off down the emergency chute. Although he declared "I quit" as he was leaving, he reversed that declaration saying that he had not resigned and sought to continue his employment by JetBlue. It takes a lot of chutzpah to carry on like that and expect to keep your job.

On a JetBlue flight in March, passengers had to restrain a pilot after his noisy eruption about al Qaeda and 9/11. The passengers have filed suit related to the incident feeling that JetBlue's offer of credit for the disrupted flight and nothing more was an insult. Their attorney says, "We know an insane pilot was flying the plane. Now we want to know why."

Also in March, a flight attendant on a Dallas to Chicago flight went berserk carrying on about 9/11 and screaming that the plane was going to crash. She was subdued by passengers one of whom said that he would never get the sound of her blood-curdling screams out of his head.

What is the cause of this irrational behavior? It used to be that the only people who acted up on planes were passengers who had had too much to drink. But when the employees go off track what are we to think?

Airline employees are under great stress. Heavier workloads, not enough sleep, job-security issues, and ill-tempered passengers, combined with unpredictable combinations of medications and alcohol to smooth out the rough spots, may be to blame for much of it. Uppers and downers, antidepressants and anti-anxiety meds are rampant, and we have no way of knowing what the person pushing the beverage cart or operating the controls in the cockpit might be *on*.

Whatever the causes, I hope they get a grip on the problem before a genuine disaster occurs that has nothing to do with terrorists, bird strikes, or mechanical failure.

*BBC America

57

Tipping

At the end of lunch with a friend the other day, she gently called my attention to the fact that, because she had paid our entire bill with a credit card – I had given her cash – the remaining money in the folder, my part of the tip, wasn't quite enough. I was grateful she mentioned it, sent for our waiter and gave him the rest of his tip in order to bring it up to twenty per cent.

None of us is especially fond of tipping in restaurants or anywhere else. But, like it or not, the tipping system is built into our culture, and there's no sign that the custom is going away any time soon.

I have long wished that the gratuity were automatically built into the check as it is in many foreign countries. That would eliminate the graceless business of postprandial calculations. But many Americans resent having to tip at all, much less pay a tip that is included in the check. Just listen to them gripe when an eighteen per cent gratuity is added to the check for tables of six or more.

They'll tell you that they don't want to be extorted into leaving a tip if they get poor service. That sounds like an excuse for being miserly, and I would suggest that those who don't like the idea of tipping perhaps shouldn't be eating in a restaurant in the first place. Restaurant dining is a luxury, not a necessity.

Most restaurant servers are paid a pitifully low wage, which I had always thought was just "the way it is" until I learned that there is a federal government category called the *sub*minimum wage that can be paid to students or trainees, people with disabilities, and tipped employees, which, of course, includes restaurant servers. And those servers, whether properly tipped or not, are required by the IRS to pay eight per cent of their tips as if they *had* received sufficient tips.

The minimum wage is $7.15. The *sub*minimum wage is $2.73, which, in theory, is supplemented by tips. But there are enough people who leave a poor tip or no tip at all to make waiting tables an iffy proposition.

Some legislators would like to see the system changed. But how, when Congress can't seem to get anything done? Should we citizens parade with picket signs in front of restaurants? Should we boycott certain restaurants to bully them into paying a decent wage? Why should they have the government's blessing?

I don't think most of us are aware of what happens to the tip we leave behind. So in case you think your waiter or waitress is pocketing the money you leave to go on a shopping spree, here, for your elucidation, is a breakdown of what happens to that gratuity:

- 3% goes to the busser, the server's most important ally
- 1% cent to the food runner, who may deliver your food but isn't your server
- 1% to the hostess
- 1.25% to the bartender, if you have consumed alcohol

An example of how horribly wrong things can go is the story of a group that ran up a $500 check in a fancy restaurant. Some of the diners were regulars. Some were not, and it was the "were nots" who paid the bill – and left a $20 tip. Because of the guidelines listed above, the waiter actually *lost* twelve dollars taking care of that table. Plus, according to IRS calculations, he would have owed forty dollars or eight per cent in taxes. And what could he say? Nothing. The servers' sanity-saving mantra has to be vent it, shrug it, let it go. The low tip was an insult, and beyond that, it was expensive.*

My husband lunches with an old high school buddy once a month. Once, the buddy mindlessly left an amount that equaled the entire amount of the check as the tip. You can imagine how thrilled the waitress was and how warmly she greeted these two elderly gentlemen on their next visit. Unfortunately for her the accidental largesse was not repeated.

My point in bringing up the subject of tipping is to emphasize, as Donna Summer sang, "They work hard for the money." And, unless the service is dreadful –

in which case the management should be made aware – they deserve every penny they get.

If you'd like an insider's peek into what goes on behind the scenes in restaurants, read Anthony Bourdain's *Kitchen Confidential*, which provides a heads up about restaurant life, Meredith Miletti's *Aftertaste: A Novel in Five Courses*, or any of several other books that might convince skeptics, who haven't given much thought to what it's like to work in a restaurant, to have a change of heart.

The holidays are approaching. So, as you're getting into the holiday spirit, don't forget that hard-working server when you're spreading around holiday cheer.

*Tipping information from www.bayareabites.com

58

I Am SO Happy

Although I love Barack Obama – he could be my son – I like Mitt Romney, too. He seems like a nice enough man, a waffler and a flip-flopper, but a nice man. He has a Norman Rockwell family – five sons, an entire regiment of grandchildren, and a wife, bless her soul, who somehow, despite daunting physical issues, persevered and survived in the meat grinder that is the American presidential campaign to support her husband. Greater love hath no woman. It just isn't possible.

Mitt Romney as President might have been bearable, although his choices for Supreme Court might not have been. Once in office he might have managed to pry loose the lunatics chewing on his ankles and become a decent, *moderate* chief executive.

But Mitt didn't win, and I am over the moon, not because I wish heartbreak on the Romneys, but because we will be spared the post-election gloating of the windbags and hatemongers who are now scrambling in vain to put a positive spin on the message that a majority of Americans have delivered to them. Among them:

- Windbag-in-Chief, Rush Limbaugh. I'm sure he's scratching his head wondering how in heaven's name he failed at rallying the forces desperate for an Obama defeat despite his relentless barrage of insults, insinuations, distortions, and just plain lies. He really should be deported. And along with him...

- Donald Trump, Jester-in-Chief, who has no business in politics in the first place and has shown his true, smarmy colors. He should be dragged to the inauguration by his hair...

- Next, the witch in blonde's clothing, Ann Coulter, and her sickening ilk, who must be apoplectic because, dammit, the *"retard"* won. Is there no God?

- The Koch brothers and Sheldon Adelson – *shame* on you Sheldon – who now know that no matter how much money you pour into a campaign you can't *buy* a president.

- Mitch McConnell: "Sorry, Mitch. Ya didn't git yer wish. Obama is a two-term president. Imagine that."

- Someone many of you have never heard or heard of, but I've heard him plenty – talk radio madman Michael Savage, who makes Limbaugh sound like Little Mary Sunshine. He's so disgusting – he hates *everyone* – that he is not permitted into the United Kingdom. Not even Limbaugh and Trump have been banned from an entire kingdom.

- Citizens United and the Supreme Court, whose efforts to purchase the presidency came to naught.

- Columnists like Jack Kelly and Charles Krauthammer whose sole *raison d'etre*, since 2008, has been to denigrate Obama.
- Perpetual mischief-makers Karl Rove and Grover Norquist.
- All of the racists, masters of dissembling – who, me racist? – who deny that they hate Obama because of his race. C'mon, people, we're not *that* naïve.
- Those whose nefarious Voter ID scheming didn't work.

Despite the vast amounts of money and energy expended to cast their father out of office, Sasha and Malia were able to go to sleep early on November 7th knowing that their father's presidency wasn't just a blip on the radar of history. The fact that he was re-elected is, if possible, more significant than the fact that he was elected in 2008. The people have spoken, again.

When you reach my age, you realize you might not be around to witness another presidential election. That's why I am *so* happy this one turned out the way it did.

Republicans, you didn't get your way. Perhaps stewing in your own juices for a while will enable you to skim off the poisons that have polluted, hijacked your party and come to your senses, so that by 2016 you can put forth a candidate who won't be torn limb from limb by internal divisions. Perhaps Republican unity can be achieved. If it isn't achievable, at least it's something to strive for.

59

What Price Integrity?

I recently read an interesting work of non-fiction, *Joseph Anton:A Memoir,* by Salman Rushdie. Who, you might wonder, is Joseph Anton, and why is Salman Rushdie writing a book about him?

I was a good way into the book before the answer was revealed. *Joseph Anton,* the first names of two of Rushdie's favorite authors, Joseph Conrad and Anton Chekhov, was the alias he chose when the Iranians, or more precisely the Ayatollah Khomeini, placed on the author a *fatwa,* a death order, on Valentine's Day 1989, following the publication of his novel *The Satanic Verses.* Radical Muslims disapproved the book's contents, considering its subject matter blasphemous to Islam. And although it is generally believed that the Ayatollah never read the book, in his milieu such a fine point would have been considered irrelevant. He believed what his lackeys told him.

Although the *fatwa* was more or less lifted in 1998, as recently as September of this year one of the pesky imams decided that it should be declared anew because, had Rushdie been properly dispensed with in the first place, others such as the creator of the film "Innocence of Muslims," initially thought to have ignited the Benghazi killings, would have been discouraged from creating blasphemous works. Said Hassan Sanei, a member of the Expediency Discernment Council, whatever that is, "I am adding another $500,000 to the reward for killing Salman Rushdie, and anyone who carries out this sentence will receive the whole amount immediately." And to think – this has been going on four twenty-four years.

Although Rushdie was born in India, because of the disapproval of Indian Muslims, *The Satanic Verses* was banned in his own country, which he was forbidden to enter for many years. As a citizen of Great Britain, he received round-the-clock protection from British police personnel, at staggering expense, which did not go down well with many Brits. And for fear of what his presence might engender, he was forbidden from flying most commercial airlines including British Airways and Lufthansa. And he was unwelcome in many countries, even to receive important literary awards.

I have not read *The Satanic Verses*, other than excerpts. But I don't need to read it in its entirely to wonder why a work of fiction is considered so wicked that legions of the offended have spent so many years and so much money and energy plotting the author's destruction. That they haven't yet succeeded is a miracle.

And I have to wonder why an author would write something that he must have suspected would rile a substantial portion of the world's population. But on the other hand, why should a writer or artist not be free to create what he or she likes? Should they be more judicious in their choice and treatment of subject matter or would that be to capitulate to the merchants of terror? Should the radicals be allowed the last word? Where does integrity leave off and foolhardiness begin?

Rushdie's friends and associates during his years of "imprisonment" fell into two categories, those who unflinchingly supported him, and those who turned their backs on him out of fear. And fear was not an irrational reaction. Although assassins haven't succeeded in killing Rushdie, they have attacked, seriously injured, and even killed others associated with translating or publishing the book.

Entire governments have cowered in the face of the *fatwa* and important individuals, who should have known better, abandoned their principles. The archbishop of Canterbury, George Carey, attacked *The Satanic Verses* and its author. The novel, Carey said, was an "outrageous slur" on the Prophet Muhammad. "We must be more tolerant of Muslim anger," the archbishop declared.

The issue raised, of course, is freedom of speech and freedom of expression. We are discouraged from yelling "Fire!" in a crowded theater, and we can be sued for certain kinds of utterances against another person. But shouldn't we otherwise, as citizens of a free society, be free to say or write what we wish?

I never expect to find myself in the rarified milieu of world-class authors that Rushdie occupies, but if I had a friend whose life was in danger because of something he had written, what would I do? Would I stand by him for the duration despite danger to myself, or would I conveniently find myself otherwise occupied?

I think I know the answer.

60

Is It Worth the Risk?

By the time you read this, the Pittsburgh Steelers 2012 season will be a distant memory, and probably not a pleasant one. We'll know whether Ben Roethlisberger was able to come back after missing part of the season not only because of a shoulder injury but because the risk to his aorta from an earlier rib injury was too great.

We'll know if Troy Polamalu was ever deemed well enough to take the field in 2012, how second-string quarterback Charlie Batch fared after it became clear to him and the rest of us that Mike Tomlin was going to send him onto the field only if Charlie Brown wasn't available.

Ten years ago I wouldn't have given a hoot about any of it. Then I decided to learn enough about the game to understand what my husband was talking about at the dinner table – or why he was taking the name of the Lord in vain in the TV room. I read a little of Joe Theismann's *The Complete Idiot's Guide to Football,* which immediately qualified me to second-guess the quarterback, the coach, and the referees, and ask a lot of stupid questions.

Since then, I've begun looking forward to the games; in fact, I jot the game times in red in my little schedule book, hoping that not too many of my "Tasteful Lady" activities will interfere with my watching the Sunday gridiron brawl. Although the December 9th game against the San Diego Chargers was so pathetic that a nap seemed like a better use of my time.

When I first started watching the games, cringing was my reaction when the players collided. Padding or not, I still don't understand how they are able to crash to the ground or into each other without breaking bones on every play. We know how we feel when we slip and fall just once.

But they *do* get hurt, as evidenced by the fact that the Steelers were playing at a fraction of their capacity the entire season because so many players were out with injuries. No athlete goes into football without being aware that it is a dangerous sport, and perhaps we should grudgingly admire their courage as we do the courage of the young men and women who sign up to go to war.

In a better-late-than-never development, retired players, officials, and owners have begun addressing the subject of injuries, especially head injuries that have not only left players permanently befuddled or disabled, but have been responsible for premature death and even suicide. According to *Time* magazine, four thousand ex-players and fifteen-hundred of their wives and children are suing the NFL for "deliberately ignoring and actively concealing" information about concussions for decades.

Be that as it may, the fans don't think much about these things. They'll weave about in their black and gold war paint, waving their Terrible Towels, until the very last player is taken from the field on a gurney.

In a recent *New York* magazine article titled "Is Football Wrong?" Will Leitch writes, "We enjoy the NFL because we can forget what goes on behind the scenes, the brutal things these players do and put themselves through." And he adds, "Can an intelligent, engaged, socially conscious person put the way he sees the world in every other context aside because he enjoys watching the games on Sunday?"

That's a good question, and by the time I finished the article I had decided that I was going to stop being part of the problem, that I wasn't going to watch this entertainment for Neanderthals ever again. I showed the article to my husband certain that he would agree and join me in my boycott. Fat chance.

That was in August. By the time September arrived, my resolve had begun to dissolve, and I found myself ensconced in front of the TV on September 9, as the pre-game hypemeister bellowed, "Are you ready for some *football?*" Millions of us were, although Will Leitch writes that "99.999 per cent of the millions who watch every Sunday couldn't say the name of a single play." I'm glad I have so much company.

The season of shortening days, cooling temperatures, and falling leaves had arrived. It was the season of football, and I appreciated having this national obsession to keep life exciting as summer's days were torn from the calendar.

I know that like the thrill-seekers in the Coliseum, I am thrilling to this carnage, physical and mental, by which I should be repelled. I am the person who shops at Wal-Mart despite misgivings about its labor practices and its bulldozer effect on small-town America. My justification is that my not shopping there won't drive them out of business. And with football I rationalize that my not watching the games won't accomplish anything of substance as the shadows lengthen, the chilly winds of autumn rattle my windows, and January's gloom lurks around the corner.

But the question remains: Is it worth the risk?

61

It Might Be Earlier Than You Think

Enjoy yourself, it's later than you think.
Enjoy yourself, while you're still in the pink.
The years go by as quickly as a wink.
Enjoy yourself, enjoy yourself,
It's later than you think.

The song "Enjoy Yourself" by Carl Sigman and Herb Magidson became a huge hit when it was recorded by Guy Lombardo in 1950, the year my father turned fifty-five. Although he had begun to contemplate his mortality, this man who was born in 1895 had another thirty years to worry about when his time would come. My mother, who was fifteen years younger, lived strong for another fifty-four years until she departed this mortal coil at ninety-four.

We all reach the point when it occurs to us that our time is running out. Of course it's running out. It started running out the day we emerged from the womb. And by now we may be further along life's continuum than we'd like to be. But we must remind ourselves of the many who haven't made it as far as we have. Reaching the end of one's life is not the exclusive province of the elderly. But have you noticed lately how the numbers in the obits are rising?

According to recent studies, there are nearly eighty thousand centenarians in the US and close to a half million world-wide. And there's a small number, super-centenarians, who live to be a hundred ten or more. Irene Ciuffoletti, who lives at the St. Anne's Home in Greensburg, Pennsylvania, celebrated her 110th birthday on January 18 with a fluffy new hairdo, a colorful cake, and a roomful of well-wishers.

How do we account for this increasing longevity? For sure, expanding medical knowledge and improvements in treatment play a role. We have an eighty-six-year-old friend who recently underwent surgery for the removal of a malignant kidney tumor the size of a cantaloupe. She was in good health otherwise and came through with flying colors. Many factors contributed to her ability to tolerate the assault on her body, but the main reason she did so well was because of her attitude – her optimism, her resilience, her joy in living, and her sense of humor. She had the nurses at the hospital chuckling the evening of her surgery.

Changes in the attitude of the medical profession were also working in her favor. Time was when they might not have considered performing major surgery on such an elderly person. But now, even those who live to a ripe old age can be granted a new lease on life by the medical establishment.

Besides a positive attitude, heredity, interest in what's going on in the world, and learning new things are life extending. But the factors that may give us the best advantage in the longevity game, as much as any of the foregoing, are diet and exercise.

My elderly husband, who is in excellent overall health, suffers from a hereditary muscular neuropathy, Charcot-Marie-Tooth Disease, in which certain muscles, in his case the leg muscles, begin to atrophy in middle age. His mother and sister were victims of Charcot and his middle-aged daughter has begun to exhibit signs of the condition.

Like any other chronic condition, Charcot worsens with age. But rather than sitting around feeling defeated, my hero has worked valiantly to delay its effects. Although at this stage he uses a walker, he performs an hour-long exercise regimen several days a week. Stretches, sit-ups and push-ups, weight-lifting, walking (slowly) on our treadmill, and pedaling our stationary bike keep his upper body strong, his weight under control, and his mind sharp. He could do as well as the young contestants on *Jeopardy!* but for the fact that he knows next to nothing about pop culture.

His attitude reminds me of the story about violinist Itzhak Perlman, who wears leg braces. He broke a string at the beginning of a concerto. But instead of waiting for a new string to be brought to him or struggling offstage to get one, he went on to play the entire piece with the three remaining strings. The lesson? Do the best you can with what you have *left*.

The late ragtime pianist and "Entertainer" composer Eubie Blake, who was a heavy smoker but lived to be a hundred, was among several wits who said, "If I'd known

I was going to live this long I'd have taken better care of myself." Funny, but also something to think about.

It would be wise for us to take better care of ourselves. It's never too late. We might have more time remaining than we think as new miracle treatments are being developed daily, and as we learn more about the benefits of good nutrition.

Nothing is guaranteed. A friend of ours, who exercised regularly and chose items exclusively from the heart-healthy menu, couldn't stop pancreatic cancer from taking her away at the age of fifty-seven.

But in today's *Post-Gazette* obits, there are several people in their nineties including one who hung it up at ninety-nine, and another who made it past the hundred year mark.

So – enjoy yourself
It's *earlier* than you think
Enjoy yourself, you *are* still in the pink
Although the days pass quickly as a wink
Enjoy yourself, enjoy yourself,
It's *earlier* than you think.

62

Spare Me Fifty Shades

I have to say that after reading the Amazon sample of E. L. James's *Fifty Shades of Grey,* the unprecedented success of this series is a phenomenon that stumps me.

On a recent NPR books podcast I learned from correspondent Lynn Neary, in an interview with Elena Legeros from the marketing department of Random House, that because of the extraordinary sales of *Fifty Shades of Grey* during 2012, every single employee of the company received a five thousand dollar year-end bonus. Imagine that, for a book that was originally a self-published, fan-fiction spin-off of the *Twilight* series, with the names and location changed. Legeros said that books like the *Fifty Shades of Grey* series are known as "miracle publications." The next closest big seller trilogy was Stieg Larsson's *Girl* series, beginning with *The Girl with the Dragon Tattoo.*

But no series of books has sold more copies in a shorter window of time than *Fifty Shades of Grey.* A Random House PR spokesman says, "It took us four years to sell twenty million copies of the *Girl* series. It took us only nine *months* to sell thirty-five million copies of the *Fifty Shades* trilogy.

Not finding books heavily laced with sado-masochism the least bit tempting, I wasn't one of the thirty-five million. And I'm at a loss to understand why there is suddenly so much interest in and acceptance of something that was, until recently, considered repugnant by the mainstream. But I'm obviously in the minority. According to Random House, resisters are few and far between.

Neary acknowledges being a prude, and she and Legeros suggest that those who wouldn't bother with *Fifty Shades*, including book store clerks and librarians, are either prudes or snobs. I deny being either. My recent reading list has included novels and non-fiction books that have social or literary merit. But I've also read some pretty free-wheeling books by Chelsea Handler, Rachel Dratch and Joan Rivers, and I doubt if any prude could get through two pages of Joan Rivers' *I Hate Everyone...Starting with Me* without losing their religion – or their lunch.

When I read the sample of *Fifty Shades of Grey*, I was struck from page one by how lame the *writing* is. Evidently I wasn't far off in my assessment. Critics aren't crazy about *Fifty Shades* either. Jo Bryant of the *Seattle Post-Intelligencer* writes, "There is so much wrong with this book that I don't know where to begin. But, if you're tempted to read it, let me warn you: It is a wasted couple of hours that you will NEVER get back. Go to the dentist instead."

The first reader review on Amazon, titled "Did a Teenager Write This?" says: "I really don't like writing bad reviews, but about half way through the book, I looked up the author to see if she is a teenager, because the characters are out of a sixteen-year-old's fantasy. The twenty-six-year-old main male character is a drop dead gorgeous billionaire – not a millionaire but a billionaire – who speaks fluent French, is a concert-level pianist, a fully trained pilot, tall, athletic, perfectly built, sexually well-endowed, and the best lover on the planet. In addition, he's not only self-made but is using his money to combat world hunger. It seems as if two teenage girls got together, decided to create their 'dream man' and came up with Christian Grey. The characters are unbelievable, and the sex scenes verge on the comical."

Another Amazon reviewer asks, "Best seller? Really? I enjoy erotica and heard so much about this book that I had to give it a shot. But I'm five chapters into it and can't take any more. This has to be the most atrocious writing I've ever seen in a major release."

There are a mind-boggling 15,816 reviews on Amazon, many of them negative, which accounts for the fact that the Amazon star rating for this juggernaut is a mere three-and-a-half out of a possible five.

Although *Fifty Shades of Grey* is not aimed at my demographic, Elena Legeros sent a copy to her grandmother in Iowa thinking that she and her friends would get a kick out of it. "Why your grandmother?" Neary asks incredulously. "Because I know what she enjoys reading and I know what a lot of the people in her assisted living home enjoy reading." Who says that residents of assisted living facilities don't get their jollies from more than arts and crafts?

Sales of grey neckties are through the roof in menswear departments, and rope and masking tape are flying off the shelves of hardware stores, thanks to the number of female shoppers who walk through the door and head straight to the hardware department.

So, considering the sales of books, an assortment of related items plus numerous parodies –not to mention those five-thousand-dollar bonuses – an awful lot of people are benefiting from *Fifty Shades of Grey* via fifty shades of *green*.

63

February 2013

What Shall We Have for Dinner?

I should be profoundly grateful that in a world where millions of hungry people would be happy to have such a problem, what to serve for dinner is the most pressing dilemma I face on a daily basis. And I know I'm not alone.

And I am grateful that whereas many women have finicky husbands whose long list of food dislikes is frustrating, and where some husbands would hurl a plate of fried eggs at their wives if the eggs weren't done to their liking, the fact that my husband enjoys my cooking, eats nearly everything I serve him, and usually compliments the meals I prepare, makes me lucky indeed.

But the question remains: What shall we have for dinner? I am often wondering about tomorrow's dinner in the middle of tonight's dinner.

This isn't a problem for those who don't cook, who eat takeout or dine in restaurants every night. But I'm of the old school and feel a responsibility as a housewife to put dinner on the table. (Feminists, have at me if you wish.)

It is staggering to contemplate that having served some semblance of dinner daily for more than forty years – when not traveling, invited to someone's home, or dining in a restaurant – by conservative estimate I have thought up more than nine thousand dinner menus. No wonder I'm exhausted.

Just in the nick of time a profusion of prepared foods has become available, frozen and fresh, which are actually *good*, can be popped into the microwave for a few minutes and are possibly tastier than a similar dish I would spend an entire afternoon organizing instead of doing more interesting things.

Gone are the days when the Swanson TV Dinner was about the only meal you could find in the supermarket freezer. They were painfully basic, and considered revolutionary at the time, although we wouldn't have dreamed of serving them to company. I've never served guests an entire meal of prepared foods, but many of them nowadays are of such quality that those who would rather munch on broken glass than host a dinner party might be induced to reconsider.

When I do prepare an entire meal from scratch, I often do so with leftovers in mind. I never serve leftovers more than one night except meatloaf, because my husband can't seem to get enough of it. If I didn't keep an eye on him he would eat meatloaf three nights in a row interspersed with meatloaf sandwiches for lunch. The recipe I use, by the way, is Martha's Mother's Meatloaf, easily accessed online. The Martha is, of course, Martha Stewart.

The freezer is a boon for those who enjoy leftovers. Casseroles and other multi-serving dishes, plus the beloved meatloaf, sliced turkey and roast beef, and individual containers of spaghetti sauce, soups and chili, are great candidates for the freezer. Once in a while I forget to label them and pull out several rock-hard packages of mystery food. "If you want to know what we're having for dinner, dear, you'll have to wait 'til it defrosts."

Trying new recipes used to be exciting – and occasionally still is. Out of curiosity I recently made Atlanta Brisket, which required the meat to be marinated for twenty-four hours in, of all things, Coca-Cola It finally dawned on me that it's called Atlanta Brisket because Atlanta is the home of Coca-Cola. The brisket was delicious, tender with plenty of sauce, but when I make it again I'll sauté some minced garlic along with the sliced onions. There's not much, other than maybe a banana split, that can't be improved by a little garlic.

In recent years I've become a little gun-shy because American fare has expanded to include all manner of ethnic foods. And after buying a little jar of this ingredient and a little box of that ingredient – never to be used again – I'm reluctant to try recipes that require an output of cash for a spice or an herb that will grow moldy or lose its flavor after languishing in my spice cabinet waiting to be used again. There is a box of Indian garam masala that has been in there for at least ten years. Evidently the tandoori chicken, or whatever delicacy I was attempting, turned out not to be a keeper.

Some recipes are intimidating at first glance. If they call for twenty ingredients and take several hours to prepare, my anxiety level rises along with my eyebrows. I've served a Jewish girlfriend a few new dishes that she and her husband loved. But she always asks me how much of a *putchke* it is. In other words, how much trouble is it to put this dish together? If it sounds to her like too much of a *putchke*, no matter how much she likes it, she will not be asking for the recipe.

Whatever the tribulations of the everyday cook may be, and no matter how many disasters go down the drain, the fact that we have a bounteous supply of foods to choose from and the means to acquire them is a wonderful thing.

And when all is said and done, despite years of head scratching and menu planning, grumbling along the way, I have to acknowledge that the most satisfying part of the day is when dinner is finally on the table and we sit down to enjoy a home-cooked meal, and perhaps a glass of wine, with family or friends.

Anyone for meatloaf?

64

Downton...Absent

At the startling conclusion of this season's *Downton Abbey*, with Matthew Crawley lying in a ditch, eyes open, blood coursing from his temple, I asked my husband, "Is he *dead?*" He answered, "Yes," to which I replied, "Oh my, there's going to be a lot of talk about *this* tomorrow at the water cooler."

All I could think of was how Lady Mary will react to the loss of her husband within mere minutes of the birth of their first child. Watching Matthew, delirious with joy, tearing along a narrow country lane in his roadster, I thought, "This is *not* going to end well." And within seconds a truck came barreling at him from the opposite direction.

Mouth agape, I had to remind myself – as if I'd been watching a horror film – these people aren't *real*. They're *made up characters*.

Creator Julian Fellowes knows how to entice us with his kaleidoscopic plotlines, and we fall for them – cliché alert – hook, line, and sinker. And to snatch *Downton Abbey* from us, just as we were getting settled in, when, among other twists, there are now *two* single-parent babies, is the "most unkindest cut" of the television season. (Shakespeare could get away with using double superlatives.)

I have to confess that after watching three seasons of this upper crust British soap opera, my husband and I still can't identify, by name, many of the characters. There are so many it is impossible to keep them straight. Twenty-four regular characters, upstairs and downstairs, and thirty-nine recurring and guest actors are a lot of names to remember.

One of those, an antagonist to the Dowager Countess, played by Maggie Smith, is Martha Levinson, mother of Lady Grantham, played by Shirley MacLaine. She has shown up only once so far, and thank heaven for that. Shirley MacLaine has her place in the world of acting, but, in my opinion, it is *not* at Downton Abbey. Whatever they were aiming for with her intrusion, I say, "Get thee back to the USA and let us be."

Among the characters whose names we know for sure are Lord and Lady Grantham, Lady Mary, Carson the butler, and the Dowager Countess Violet, who, in the eyes of many, steals the show with her imperious bearing and judiciously placed zingers.

Maggie Smith, interviewed on *60 Minutes* the evening of the season's last episode, says that she has never watched an episode of *Downton Abbey*. For her, the pleasure is in the acting. At seventy-eight, I hope she sticks around long enough to watch herself demolish everyone whose behavior or opinions displease her, while many of us are thinking something like, "Go, girl," that crude Americanism that would give the Dowager

Countess the vapors and is utterly incongruous with the hoity-toity goings-on at Downton Abbey.

Perhaps you are aware that NBC turned down *Downton Abbey*, believing that American audiences would not have an appetite for a British historical drama set in a country manor in Edwardian England. Reflecting on their lack of vision, the network honchos must be astounded and chagrined by the show's monster success.

In truth, however, it probably would have been a mistake to put *Downton Abbey* on network television. There are many who watch PBS who never go near network television. Plus, a PBS berth gives the show a cachet it could never achieve on NBC.

The NBC execs have forgotten or never knew about the extraordinary success of the award-winning Masterpiece Theater series *Upstairs, Downstairs*, which ran for sixty-eight episodes, from 1971-75. It involved a similarly aristocratic family, the Bellamys, during the same era, and had much the same flavor. *Upstairs, Downstairs* was "must see TV" on Sunday nights and was just as much discussed on Monday mornings.

But many *Downton Abbey* fans weren't yet born when *Upstairs, Downstairs* pioneered the upstairs/downstairs prime time concept. And, to my surprise, practically nothing has been written about it during the *Downton Abbey* hysteria.

I recently watched a few episodes of *Upstairs, Downstairs* to see how it holds up to *Downton Abbey*. Along with the splendor of its settings, *Upstairs, Downstairs* had the added presence of the handsome and urbane

Alistair Cook to brief us on what we were about to see. Current host of *Masterpiece*, Laura Linney, is a fine actress, but no one, including Russell Baker, who hosted for a time, could replace Alistair Cook.

Alas, we must content ourselves with commoners – through spring, summer, fall and another winter – before we can hie to that grand Edwardian manor, known in real life as Highclere Castle, but ever in our imaginations as *Downton Abbey*.

65

A Hopeless Case

There are things we *must* do in life and there are things we *should* do. We must pay taxes, we must shovel our sidewalks to keep from being sued, and we must take a shower every week or so or risk being shunned by our friends. Among the things we *should* do is exercise. I do not enjoy exercise. I find it an ordeal. And despite several decades of noble intentions, I'm resigned to the fact that I cannot stick to an exercise routine, and I've given up on all but the paltriest of efforts.

In a brief flirtation with yoga, I didn't find it the panacea others do. I tried tai chi but must have been doing it wrong because I blew out my left knee. And for a few weeks I went to a personal trainer in Shadyside. After a month of driving to Shadyside in all kinds of traffic I put a stop to that. Why did I go all the way to Shadyside? Good question. The trainer was either highly recommended or awfully good looking.

At the suggestion of a physical therapist, I joined a facility with a swimming pool so that I could attend water aerobics classes. Sounded like a super idea, so I went to Macy's, bought a bathing suit, rubber flip-flops, a big fluffy towel, and a satchel to tote around my "gear."

I went to the class. Once. The place isn't far from home, but the prospect of driving there, disrobing, struggling into the suit, doing the kick and splash routine, and then doing it all in reverse was something I did not look forward to doing several times a week. I haven't been back, and when I do give it a moment's thought, the thought is that I *will* go back – when the weather's warmer, when I'm not so busy, right before I get my hair done, or when they begin serving hot fudge sundaes in the lobby. It doesn't help that the class meets at 1 p.m. Don't they realize that's when I'm lunching with my friends?

We're all aware that regular exercise gives us strength and flexibility, keeps our weight under control, and improves our cardio-vascular health and feelings of well-being by raising endorphin levels, prolonging life in general.

But despite knowing all that, the only exercise I manage to perform on a regular basis is twenty minutes on the treadmill and Power Rider in our basement for the purpose of burning calories. The TV is on, but what I'm really watching is the clock. And when those twenty minutes are up my conscience is clear and I can enjoy my day with that tedious obligation out of the way.

On a recent two-week cruise I got myself onto the fitness center's rowing machine for three twenty-minute sessions, which burned up several hundred calories. But how many calories did I consume with two weeks of Eggs Benedict, raisin-cinnamon buns – with butter – and four-course gourmet dinners?

Ever the optimist, I tried Pilates. "It strengthens your core," they told me, and heaven knows my core needed strengthening. I found a lovely trainer, an energetic young woman who had spent several years dancing in cruise ship shows. And we know how limber and svelte those ladies have to be. I faithfully showed up for my lessons, but they were so exhausting that I gave up with one paid-for session left in my series.

As a member of Silver Sneakers, I can exercise free of charge at most of the health clubs in the area. I found an attractive one in Moon Township, World Class Fitness. Since you can't get much classier than world class, I signed up with renewed optimism, figuring it was well worth the twenty-five minute drive from home. A trainer took me through the weight and strengthening room, showed me a routine of exercises, and I was ready to tighten my abs and buns all the way back to the '60s, when I was young and taut. I went maybe four times, but I was so sore the next day, after those half-hours of pumping iron, I could hardly lift a glass of water to take a pain pill. So, despite the fact that they have world class equipment and their treadmills are equipped with touch-screen TV's, I bid my World Class rehabilitation adieu.

Because aerobics doesn't seem so much like exercise, I find it the most palatable form of exertion. I love to dance and what is aerobics if not dancing? A couple of decades ago I passed a course at a nearby YMCA to become a certified aerobics instructor. But I've yet to teach a class. My bright idea was to develop an aerobics program using classical music. But when I found out it would be a hassle to get permission to use recorded music, I couldn't see spending half my time at my desk navigating usage issues when I should be doing aerobics or walking around the high school track.

I know I have plenty of company in my aversion to exercise. We all know we should do it and have the best of intentions, but there are so many other activities that are more interesting or fun or useful that we can do sitting down, or at least standing still. So I'm reconciled to being part of the majority who would rather lift a fork than a barbell.

But y'know? My dear mother lived to be a fairly robust ninety-four and never exercised a whit unless you consider running up and down the stairs lugging baskets of laundry, mopping the kitchen floor with Soilax, ironing cotton sheets and shirts, and walking to and from the market with a whiney little kid and heavy bags of groceries, exercise. She was from a generation when being a housewife was all the exercise she needed.

66

A Day on the Learning Curve

For my husband's birthday I decided to give him a new TV with a bigger screen and clearer picture. Our aging eyes would be better able to read the subtitles of the foreign movies we enjoy via Netflix, and we'd have a clearer view of the Steelers having their brains pulverized during the upcoming season.

The new set was delivered the day after his birthday. Little did we know that big troubles were about to start courtesy of, among other things, a connector called HDMI or High-Definition Multimedia Interface.

It's been a while since we've bought a new TV, and neither of us had the slightest idea that HDMI is now the standard way of hooking up certain components to a TV set. And after several hours of fiddling around with cables and ports, it became apparent that our old reliable TiVo video recorder was incompatible with the new TV.

So, with little interest in spending more money but even less in sending back the new TV, off I went to buy a new TiVo, which to my complete surprise, is now accessed, rather than by telephone line, by wireless adapter. Uh-oh.

I'll spare you some of what followed my well-meaning decision to buy a new TV. But I will tell you that I have since spent countless hours on the phone with a battalion of technical support people (most of whom speak English I can actually understand). The problem is that to get the new system working the way it should, four devices have to be functioning properly: the modem, which is attached to the desktop computer and needed for Internet access; the router – which transmits Wi-Fi signals; a range extender, which reinforces and redirects weak Wi-Fi signals from the router to the wireless devices in our TV room – the TiVo wireless adapter, and ROKU – a little box that lets us stream movies from Netflix and other sources.

Each of these devices, from four different manufacturers, requires calling a different support person. And, because they can only advise you about their own company's products, you are given incomplete or incorrect instructions but have no way of knowing that at the time. That's when a conference call would come in handy.

My day of instruction begins with an order to unplug the Ethernet cable – the one that looks like an overgrown telephone jack – from my computer, so that I can plug another device into it. This requires me to dive under my desk, and because it's as dark as a cave under there, I run off to find a flashlight. Back under the desk, I locate the Ethernet cable, and make the switch, the whole time wondering what effect all of this plugging and unplugging will have on my new manicure.

For the next six hours, up and down and back and forth I go, even once speaking into the TV remote and wondering why the person on the other end wasn't saying anything.

The entire time all of this frantic activity is going on, my husband is sitting at the kitchen table, reading the morning paper, watching me run back and forth with the telephone, like the Road Runner, between the den (TV room) and my office, a distance of seventy feet, following instructions. "Hook up this." "Unplug that." "Restart your computer." "Unplug the adapter and wait twenty seconds." I wait twenty seconds. "Should I plug it back in now?" I ask. "Yes," (you idiot) she's thinking.

The situation becomes so dire that following a TiVo instruction requires me to burst into the den while my husband is meditating. I *never* go into the den while he's meditating. But understanding fellow that he is, he later tells me that he was expecting such an intrusion, and that when I left he quickly sank back into his trance.

I wonder what my friends, who assume I have a modicum of dignity, would think if they saw me engaged in this technical-support marathon. Most would never subject themselves to it. Those who watch little or no television would think it serves me right. And those who are more technically savvy than I would just roll their eyes and bask in their superiority.

The system is up and running now, but I'm holding my breath. When I least expect it a "You are not connected to the Internet" message will appear on the TV screen, and back to my knees I'll fall, saying a couple of prayers while I'm down there.

I must say that the support people are unfailingly polite as they put me through my paces and might be surprised to know that the woman on the other end, huffing and puffing through the house and diving under her desk every two minutes, is old enough to be their grandmother.

And as far as wireless devices are concerned, I can only laugh when I look at the cluster of cables and cords under my desk and behind the TV. It appears that the only device around here that functions well without being plugged into a wall is my husband.

67

How Will This Decade Make Its Mark?

Considering the fact that, contrary to previous interpretations of the Mayan calendar, the world as we know it did *not* come to an end on December 21, 2012, I find myself wondering what events or developments will define the current decade.

Some decades have a personality so distinct that they acquire sobriquets such as "The Gay Nineties," "The Roaring Twenties," and "The Sixties," which was such an extraordinary decade that, shell-shocked, we spent the next twenty years reconciling ourselves to the fact that our culture had been turned inside out.

In the 1990s, technology forever changed the way we communicate and gather information. By way of the World Wide Web, the Internet made instant global communication available to the masses, and the tech bubble produced a small explosion of baby billionaires like Bill Gates, who became moguls before they turned thirty-five. Until they came along, we thought of billionaires as cigar-chomping captains of industry like J. P. Morgan and Andrew Carnegie.

The first decade of this century will be remembered for two world-changing events, 9/11 and the election of Barack Obama. Some tried to label the decade the "Oughts," or the "Aughts," but – and we can all be grateful for this – neither epithet ever caught on. Name or no name, we won't be forgetting those ten years any time soon.

I began to ponder why certain decades make a deeper impression on history than others because of the popularity of recent books and movies, and a TV series, all of which are set in the 1920s. *Midnight in Paris* and *The Artist* take us back to that period, just after World War I, when the shackles of Victorianism had been cast aside and replaced by the Roaring Twenties, which were like a dam let loose, inundating us with jazz, talkies, the flappers, cars for the masses, a profusion of creative output, and that worst experiment in the history of mankind, Prohibition. The television series *Boardwalk Empire*, gives us a glimpse of the chaos that ensued when the sale of alcoholic beverages was made illegal.

A current novel by Paula McLain, *The Paris Wife*, tells the story of Ernest Hemingway through the eyes of his first wife, Hadley Richardson. Set mostly in Paris in the '20s, their world was populated by the creative geniuses of the early twentieth century – Gertrude Stein, T. S. Eliot, and F. Scott Fitzgerald. And although Prohibition might have been the law in the United States, in Paris these expatriates – the women as well as the men – drank such staggering amounts of liquor that one has to wonder how they sobered up enough to accomplish anything worthwhile.

The '20s sailed along dizzily until the stock market crash in 1929 plunged the world into the Great Depression. And it was during the '20s that Hitler began making steady progress in his quest for world domination, although nearly everyone, Americans in particular, was in denial until it was too late to stop him.

This second decade of the 2000s continues to stumble along on toddler's legs, on the way to establishing its identity. Eight years remain for it to carve its place in history. The pessimist in me fears that the signal events of the 2010s will not be happy ones considering that millions of our fellow humans are all too eager to kill themselves in order to kill us and are dedicating their lives to doing so. Nor do struggling world economies and political and cultural upheaval fuel much optimism.

Barring our annihilation, will this be remembered as the decade during which...

- We elect the first woman president?
- We conquer our dependence on foreign oil?
- Chemotherapy will become as obsolete as blood-letting?
- A drug to prevent Alzheimer's disease will be developed?
- Printed books, newspapers, and magazines will cease to exist except in archival form?
- Eye or touch recognition will render obsolete the need for identification credentials and passwords?

That's my short list. How do you think this decade will make its mark – by cultural, political, technological, or medical means? Or something as yet unimagined?

None of us has a crystal ball, but it does no harm to speculate.

Acknowledgements

The publication of this book would not have been possible without the help and encouragement of my one-in-a-million husband Charles Johnson, Robert Croan and Peter King of the *Pittsburgh Post-Gazette*, Peg Stewart of the *Green Tree Times*, a long list of fans and supporters, proofreaders extraordinaire Nancy and Miranda Santucci, and Bill Henry, who provided the wind beneath my wings to get this project off the ground.

About The Author

Until her retirement in 2006, Patricia Prattis Jennings spent more than forty years as Principal Keyboard of the Pittsburgh Symphony Orchestra, traveling the world not only as a member of the orchestra and featured soloist, but also as a soloist with numerous orchestras in the United States.

Daughter of the late P. L. Prattis, editor of the *Pittsburgh Courier,* Jennings' writing career began in 1994 when she was asked to do a four-part series, "Symphony Diary," for the *Pittsburgh Post-Gazette* during a month-long European tour. Since then she has written not only for the *Post-Gazette* but also for *Symphony* magazine (American Symphony Orchestra League), *The Phoenix* (Western Pennsylvania Mensa), the Pittsburgh *City Paper* and the *Green Tree Times.*

From 1988 to 1994 she was the editor/publisher of *Symphonium,* an influential, nationally-circulated newsletter "for and about the professional African-American symphony musician."

She and husband Charles H. Johnson, a retired retail manager, reside a few miles outside of Pittsburgh.

5040392R00177

Made in the USA
San Bernardino, CA
21 October 2013